Curiosities Series

# Vermont
# CURIOSITIES

### Quirky characters, roadside oddities & other offbeat stuff

Robert F. Wilson; photos by Victoria Blewer;
Foreword by U.S. Senator Bernie Sanders

Guilford, Connecticut

The prices, rates, and hours listed in this guidebook were confirmed at press time. We recommend, however, that you call establishments to obtain current information before traveling.

Copyright © 2009 by Morris Book Publishing, LLC

All photos by Victoria Blewer unless otherwise indicated
Text design by Bret Kerr
Maps by Daniel Lloyd @ Morris Book Publishing, LLC

Library of Congress Cataloging-in-Publication Data is available on file.

ISBN 978-0-7627-4669-9

Printed in the United States of America

10 9 8 7 6 5 4 3 2 1

To Casey, Jillian,
Willem, Isabella,
and Emma
—Stalwarts all

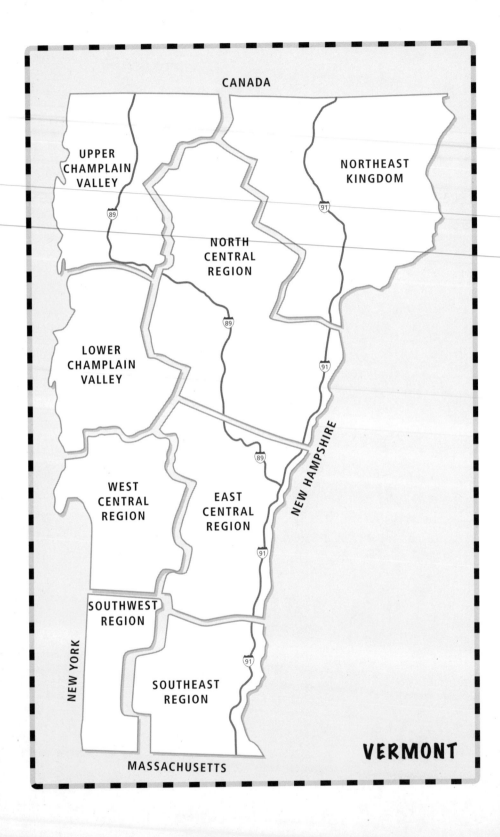

# contents

★ ★ ★ ★ ★ ★ ★ ★ ★ ★ ★ ★ ★ ★ ★ ★ ★ ★ ★ ★ ★ ★ ★ ★ ★ ★ ★ ★ ★ ★ ★ ★ ★ ★ ★ ★

# acknowledgments

Many Vermonters, as well as a few former residents from states as far away as California, have contributed to the content of this book. Suggestions from friends, colleagues, and "helpful professionals" came in welcome and diverse ways.

Several kind experts in Vermont history or sociology have suggested sources to facilitate further research. These include David Deen, state representative and steward, Connecticut River Watershed Council; Richard Ewald, Rockingham development director; Nat Frothingham, publisher, *Montpelier Bridge*; the late Graham Newell, Saint Johnsbury Academy; Prof. Robert H. Rodgers, University of Vermont; and Georgia Valentine, Vermont Historical Society.

A number of knowledgeable individuals have contributed information or source material for specific entries. Among them were Cathy Amerling; Philip Atwood; Mary Baswell; Eloise Biel, Lake Champlain Maritime Museum; Chris Bohjalian; Michael Briggs, communications director for U.S. senator Bernie Sanders; David Carle, communications director for U.S. senator Patrick Leahy; Christy Carter, Vermont State Archives; Tim Clark, Esq.; Kins Collins; Patrick Crowley, *Brattleboro Reformer*; Joseph DeMuzio; Meg Dansereau, Graton Associates, Inc.; Vincent DiBernardo, DVM; John Dodd, Castleton Town Manager; Vermont lieutenant governor Brian Dubie; Minnie Marx Eagle; Lawrence Forcier, director, Lake Champlain Sea Grant; Jack Galt, facilities director, Flynn Center for the Performing Arts; Manuel Garcia; Arnold Graton, restoration conservationist; Prof. David Howell, Stanford University; Don Keelan; Dan Libertino, president, Sikorsky Archives; Gail Nunziata, managing director, Latchis Corporation; Bob O'Connor; Scott Olson, Casella Waste Systems; Bob Paquin, aide to U.S. senator Patrick Leahy; Paula Maynard, press director, Lincoln Family Home at Hildene; Bill Senkus, Alphabetilately; Susan Shea, Green Mountain Club; Marcia Shin; Susan Smallheer, *Rutland Herald;* Rich Svec, Cavendish town manager; Bob Thomson; Ken Wells, publisher, *Newport Daily Express*; Don and Dave Trachte; Ruth Wallman, Lake Champlain Islands Chamber of Commerce; Jane Woodruff, Brookfield town clerk; and Leslie Wright, publicity and marketing manager, Shelburne Museum.

# acknowledgments

Several creative Vermonters have suggested topics or entries that were included in one or more chapters: Bob Audette, *Brattleboro Reformer*; Joe Benning, Esq.; Jed Davis, Cabot Creamery; Sue Davis, Esq; J. J. Laukaitis; Tom McPhee, Bellows Falls Selectman; Albert Neill; Warren S. Patrick; Jim Reagan; Todd Roy; Scott Wheeler, publisher, *Vermont's Northland Journal*; and John Wood.

The Major L.L.B. Angas story, in chapter 2, was a group effort, pieced together from the remarkable memories of Saxtons River residents Fred Brown, Bob Campbell, Averill C. Larsen, David Moore, and Albert Neill, with additional input from a July 27, 1940, illustrated article in *The Saturday Evening Post*.

The engraving accompanying the Phineas Gage story in chapter 5 is reprinted from the *American Journal of Medical Sciences*, n.s. v. 20 (July 1850): 13–22 Bigelow, Henry J., "Dr. Harlow's case of recovery from the passage of an iron bar through the head," courtesy of the Harvard Medical Library in the Francis A. Countway Library of Medicine.

Martha Buchanan's research of primary and secondary sources provided much of the raw data that got many entries off the ground and generated ideas for additional entries, as well.

Photographer Victoria Blewer, in addition to the numerous photos she took for the book, contributed several story ideas, including three based on interesting photos she took that themselves produced entries.

Back at Globe Pequot central, acquisitions editor Gillian Belnap was the prime mover, from concept to specific content during the initial stages of gestation. Editor Allen Jones shepherded the raw manuscript and illustrations through the editorial process from Globe Pequot's Helena, Montana, office—hand-holding and arm-twisting as necessary. Copyeditor Lillia Gajewski remedied uneasy syntax, suggested more felicitous wording and word placement, and pulled me back to safe shores when I leaned into the abyss of bad taste. Finally, project manager Gia Manalio-Bonaventura had the fun job of cleaning up the

# acknowledgments

mess the rest of us left behind, somehow bringing order to chaos and serving as a lonely voice of reason. To those I've neglected to include or have listed erroneously, I apologize. Please bring instances of such stupidity to my attention, and I'll make amends in the next edition of *Vermont Curiosities*.

# foreword

Vermont is a state of great natural beauty, of mountains and valleys, of forests and farms, of villages and vibrant small cities. The generosity of Vermont's landscape is matched by the generosity of its people.

Vermont also is a state with a long history, a history filled with innovation. Visitors to our state, as well as Vermont residents, will find *Vermont Curiosities* full of brief descriptions of Yankee ingenuity, and, since the book is organized geographically and contains plenty of roadside directions, they will learn where to find those examples of ingenuity.

Readers will, in these pages, encounter Vermont's remarkable network of 5,000 miles of snowmobile trails stretching from Canada to Massachusetts, maintained by a volunteer network known as VAST, with its 138 chapters. Readers will briefly meet Justin Morrill, the high school dropout who became a U.S. senator and established the land grant colleges of this country, opening higher education to the children of working-class families. They will find out how to visit King Arthur Flour in Norwich, which today flourishes as a wonderful example of an employee-owned company.

They'll learn about the first ski tow in America, about hang gliding, about Barre's granite quarries, about the world's longest two-span wooden bridge. They'll encounter the birth of "The Free and Independent State of Vermont" in Windsor, a year before the Constitution was ratified.

This book is an informative and pleasurable compendium to those who want to travel Vermont and see things not found in most guidebooks and will be a delight to those who enjoy the quirkiness of finding out about Vermont's "curiosities."

—Bernie Sanders
U.S. Senator

# preface

In and around the Arctic Circle, a condition called "permafrost" causes a mixture of underground moisture and soil to freeze into a concrete-like mass—sturdy enough (until recently, anyway) to support highways and three-story buildings, winter and summer, year after year. In Vermont, a bit south and slightly milder, we're lucky enough not to have such a climate. Instead, dozens of microclimates produce a winter moisture and soil combination that freezes much more randomly, causing sharp upthrusts particularly noticeable on secondary roads. Motorists quickly adapt, however, especially when alerted by road signs reading FROST HEAVES AHEAD!

This brings us to Vermont's only professional basketball team: Here's to the Frost Heaves! Any state serious enough of purpose to name an athletic team in honor of indigenous geological phenomena rather than mammals of prey earns points for originality. The team's tag line challenges upcoming opponents by evoking the origins of its name: "We're gonna be the bump in their road."

Vermont was *born* original, as you'll see in chapter 1. Pressured by New Hampshire to the east, by New York to the west, and by Massachusetts to the south to give up more and more land as colonies were being formed back in the 1700s, it declined membership as one of the first thirteen united states, deciding instead to go its own way as a sovereign nation. It finally joined the union in 1791, under more favorable terms.

Fifty years later, Rev. (and historian) Hosea Beckley noted in *The History of Vermont* that Vermonters "are not ashamed to be seen going to Boston in caps made of their own mountain fur; in striped woolens manufactured within their own dwellings; in vehicles constructed by themselves; and drawn by horses of their own raising." Residents today who come from Vermont families going back five, six, and seven generations are known for this same iconoclastic spirit. Newcomers who see something about the state and its people that makes them want to live here too, soon adapt to it—either totally or partially. Those who don't adapt usually don't stay. (Total disclosure: I'm in my second decade as a Vermonter, meaning that I'll never shed the label "Flatlander," which adheres to all inhabitants who don't yet have four generations of ancestors "in the ground." My wife, born in Alaska, at least has a face-saving comeback. I grew up in Illinois, where the highest point in my former county is Bald Mound, at 739 feet. Not much I can do about it now.)

*Vermont Curiosities* is organized geographically, the first chapter dealing with statewide matters—historical, geographical, and cultural. The remaining eight chapters cover regions delineated on the map on page vi. The remarkable people, events, and "curiosities" represented by the stories told on these pages are a mere fraction of a total, limited only by time and space. If you take a look at the acknowledgments, you'll see that this was anything but a one-man job. I had all the help I needed. All I had to do was ask.

An unlucky fellow died one day and wound up in the long line of judgment. As he waited, he noticed that some souls marched through the pearly gates straight into Heaven, while others were led over to Satan, who promptly threw them into the fires of Hell.

Every so often the man saw Satan tossing a poor soul off to one side into a small pile instead of into the fire. Finally, the man's curiosity got the better of him.

"Excuse me, Prince of Darkness," he said. "Why are you tossing those wretches aside, instead of flinging them into the fire with the others?"

"Ah, those," said Satan. "They're from Vermont. They're still too cold and wet to burn."

—Anonymous

1

## Statewide

**Some of this** state's curiosities and oddities stretch across multiple regions. The Long Trail, for example, starts in Massachusetts and scales just about every mountaintop in the way of its zigzag route to Canada. A few years after its completion, it became the inspiration for (and shared part of its route with) the better-known Appalachian Trail.

Water knows no boundaries, which is why the devastating flood of 1927 story is appropriate in this chapter.

Finally, believe it or not, Vermont was a nation before it was a state. Back in the 1600s everybody wanted a piece of this stunning real estate. Massachusetts claimed part of it. So did New York and New Hampshire. But Vermont's leaders declined membership as the four-teenth of the original colonies and decided the state should go its own way as a sovereign nation. You might say it seceded from what wasn't yet even the United States of America. And that's where we begin this curious story.

★ ★ ★ ★ ★ ★ ★ ★ ★ ★ ★ ★ ★ ★ ★ ★ ★ ★ ★ ★ ★ ★ ★ ★ ★ ★ ★ ★ ★

## The Sovereign Nation of Vermont

*"Vermont" is an English name taken from* Les Monts Verts, *which is what French explorer Samuel de Champlain called Vermont's Green Mountains on his 1647 map.*

Quick, name the original thirteen United States.

Let's see . . . Massachusetts, Connecticut, Vermont . . . Wrong! Actually, Vermont did not join the union until 1791, as the fourteenth state. In 1777, with Massachusetts, New Hampshire, and New York all trying to swallow up parts of the colony, Vermont thumbed its nose at its neighbors and everyone else and wrote its own constitution as a free and independent republic, answerable to nobody. On July 4 the constitution of Vermont was drafted at Elijah West's tavern in Windsor and adopted by the delegates on July 8 after four days of debate.

All this was due to some double-dealing by King George III. In effect King George handed over Vermont to both New Hampshire and New York. He granted New Hampshire's governor, John Wentworth, all land to within 30 miles of the Hudson River and then turned around and gave New York the land all the way to the east bank of the Connecticut River. Massachusetts jumped in and claimed some of it, too.

Between 1777 and 1791 Vermont governed itself as a sovereign entity, with the town of Windsor as its capital. It convened an elected assembly, created and operated a postal service, coined its own money, and outlawed slavery throughout the state (as the U.S. Constitution of 1787 did not do). Thomas Chittenden was its first—and only—president. During this time Vermont's militia, led by Ethan Allen (as general of the army of Vermont) and his Green Mountain Boys, successfully beat off attempts by surrounding states to annex parts of the state. In 1778 Allen was captured by the British, taken to New York, and after a few days exchanged for British colonel Archibald Campbell. In 1791 Vermont paid New York $30,000 dollars to settle all its land disputes and was admitted to the Union.

★ ★ ★ ★ ★ ★ ★ ★ ★ ★ ★ ★ ★ ★ ★ ★ ★ ★ ★ ★ ★ ★ ★ ★ ★ ★ ★ ★ ★ ★ ★

Vermont's dedication to independence has become a distinguishing characteristic. For example, that Vermont became a republic so irritated the State of Georgia that its legislature issued a proclamation saying, in part: "The whole state should be made into an island and towed out to sea." On September 29, 1941, the State of Vermont declared war on Germany—more than two months before the nation as a whole made its declaration. Most recently, in 2006, a group of dissatisfied citizens was formed, "dedicated to the proposition that Vermonters should peaceably secede from the United States and govern themselves as an independent republic once again." Now what are *these* Vermonters riled up about? For more information see www.vtcommons.org.

### The Trail That Inspired the Appalachian Trail

*A Vermont Academy headmaster gets a big idea off the ground: The oldest long-distance trail in the United States.*

The Long Trail shares a route with the younger Appalachian Trail until the two part company just north of Sherburne Center, about 100 miles north of the Massachusetts border.

# Vermont Weather Extremes

The coldest temperature ever recorded in Vermont was 50 degrees below zero Fahrenheit in Bloomfield, Essex County, on December 30, 1933. The warmest was 105 degrees Fahrenheit in Vernon in the southeast corner of the state, on July 4, 1911. The greatest amount of snow from a single storm—50 inches in three days—fell on Readsboro in Bennington County on March 2–5, 1947. The greatest snowfall total for a single season was 318.6 inches (26½ feet) in 1970–1971.

If you want to get a feel for Vermont's geography, geology, topography, flora, and fauna, here's a walk you might consider. The downside is that you'll need to set aside four to six weeks to complete it, if you want to earn "end-to-ender" status. This is the Long Trail, which follows the spine of the Green Mountains for 272 miles, from Massachusetts to Quebec.

But let's say you don't have six weeks, or need more information before you make a commitment. The Green Mountain Club, which protects and maintains the trail, has created a way to test-drive the Long Trail and learn more about the experience. Visit its headquarters (Web site and other contact information at the end of this story), talk to staff members, look over the trail guides and maps, and conquer the Short Trail, a half-mile loop and microcosm of the total experience. Now you're ready for any number of day hikes, as well.

This "footpath in the wilderness" occurred to Vermont outdoorsman James P. Taylor nearly a hundred years ago as he waited for the fog to lift during a hike on Stratton Mountain. To get things moving Taylor, assistant headmaster of Vermont Academy, in Saxtons River, founded the Green Mountain Club (GMC) in 1910 and was its first president. Over the next twenty years, a 272-mile path was cleared, hitting just about every summit along the way, from Consultation Peak near the Massachusetts border to Mount Carleton, just south of the Canadian border. Today seventy huts and shelters 8 to 10 miles apart provide overnight cover, protection from the weather, and a dry place to prepare meals. The Long Trail map identifies 185 miles of 1- to 5-mile access trails, a few of which can also serve as loop trails for day hikes. The GMC also has identified six supply stations—grocery, post office, and bar-and-grill stops at 45- to 55-mile intervals—to provide basic services and sustenance. Some 200,000 hikers trek the Long Trail yearly, and more than one hundred of them make it from end to end.

The Long Trail shares its southernmost 100 miles with the better-known Appalachian Trail. The two trails part company just north of U.S. Route 4 near Sherburne Center. The Long Trail then continues north to Canada, and the Appalachian Trail veers west to New Hampshire and Maine. The Long Trail is credited with being the inspiration for the younger, longer Appalachian Trail. Now here's a conundrum: In 1900, ten years before James Taylor's Stratton Mountain epiphany, Appalachian Trail (AT) founder Benton MacKaye claimed to have been identically inspired by a Stratton Mountain vision. Then twenty-one years went by before MacKaye published his AT proposal. Why? No one seems to know.

During its history the GMC has been vigorously proactive in preserving the wilderness character of the Long Trail. When a scenic highway the length of the Green Mountain Range was proposed in the mid-1930s, the club mounted a spirited enough opposition to cause its rejection in a statewide referendum. A planned missile communications facility on Mount Mansfield in 1958 met the same fate in the face of club resistance. The GMC has conserved more than 25,000 acres of Long Trail lands, many of which have been added to Vermont's state forests. More than 800 volunteers aid GMC staffers in keeping an eye on trails and making repairs when needed.

One of the most demanding sections of the trail is the ascent of Mount Mansfield, north of Stowe and crossing Route 108 in an area

★ ★ ★ ★ ★ ★ ★ ★ ★ ★ ★ ★ ★ ★ ★ ★ ★ ★ ★ ★ ★ ★ ★ ★ ★ ★ ★ ★ ★

known as Smugglers' Notch. Actually, Mount Mansfield claims six peaks, which together are said to resemble the head and neck of a giant in repose. (The Abenaki thought it rather the profile of a moose head. Make up your own mind when you get there.)

*Writer Bill Scheller and friend Rich Mara hike the Long Trail every year, usually in November because they have the trail and shelters all to them-selves. Following is an excerpt from Bill's account of his 2007 ascent to Mt. Mansfield's "chin," at 4,393 feet the highest point in Vermont. The complete story, "Up and Across Mt. Mansfield," appears in www.natural traveler.com (click on "Archives" to find the 11/16/07 issue).*

"The Long Trail itself, once it ascends beyond treeline at this end of Mansfield, boldly pushes itself and its plucky trekkers to the threshold of technical climbing. At several points, with the Chin summit tantalizingly within view, we were forced to ascend on hands and knees, always remembering that backpacks play havoc with one's center of gravity. One spot was particularly challenging: You had to plant your knees on a rock shelf as wide as your knees. This made for a fine puzzle, as the next thing you had to do was get a foot up onto the space already occupied by your knees, or at least one of them. I don't recall how I did it, but I remember that the alternative would have been to stay there forever like a stunted pine, or hope that a ledge ten feet below would have impeded my descent to level ground, some two hundred feet down.

"The views from the Chin were worth the little frisson of doom. From the roof of Vermont, we looked east toward Mt. Washington in New Hampshire, north past Jay Peak into Quebec's Eastern Townships, and west across lowland farms and villages to Lake Champlain and the Adirondacks beyond."

Directions: The club is about 4 miles south of Stowe on the west side of Route 100. Take the next right entrance at the sign for the 1836 Cabins and Evergreen Gardens just before the GMC office. Hours vary by season. No admission charged. For more information visit www.greenmountainclub.org or call (802) 244-7037.

## Trivia

### Vermont—Most Rural State in the Nation

The definition of "rural" depends upon the number of people who reside in places with fewer than 2,500 people. Because most of the 255 cities, towns, and gores in which Vermonters live have fewer than 2,500 residents, the state is by definition rural. Services and elected officials usually follow these local boundaries. Unlike most states, in which counties are the unit used to determine rural and urban populations, Vermont's fourteen counties are organized only to provide law enforcement and judicial services. No other governmental services exist at the county level.

### The Flood That Changed a State

Vermonters were looking for relief after evenly spaced storms in October 1927 thoroughly saturated the state. Instead, on November 2, a storm from the mid-Atlantic coast met yet another from the upper Great Lakes region. A high-pressure area over the state of Maine effectively held these two storms motionless over Vermont. The result was a drenching that lasted forty-five consecutive hours. During that time nearly 10 inches of rain fell.

Virtually every river and stream violently overflowed its banks. Nearly 1,300 bridges were washed away. Railways and highways disappeared. Eighty-four people lost their lives. More than 9,000 were left homeless, 15,000 cattle drowned, and the total cost in property losses was $700 million in today's dollars. Eight thousand

★ ★ ★ ★ ★ ★ ★ ★ ★ ★ ★ ★ ★ ★ ★ ★ ★ ★ ★ ★ ★ ★ ★ ★ ★ ★ ★ ★ ★

Vermonters were given food, clothing, shelter, and medical assistance.

The northern half of the state was particularly hard hit. Author R. E. Atwood, in a book published just six weeks later, was inspired to anthropomorphic heights: "As if drunk with its new-found power," Atwood wrote, "the Winooski River staggered and roared its crooked way down the valley, ripping out trees, tearing away houses, barns, bridges, and gathering livestock and even human beings into is awful arms until spent with its Herculean effort, it passed mutteringly out into Lake Champlain."

Earlier that year President Calvin Coolidge had taken considerable heat for his lack of effort in response to an even more horrendous flood. When the Mississippi River burst through dozens of levees in every border state south of Illinois, 700,000 were estimated to have lost their homes, and the death toll reached 246. Even so, President Coolidge refused to visit the area, and declined to broadcast an appeal for relief funds on national radio.

Stung by the criticism, Coolidge appointed Commerce Secretary Herbert Hoover to be in charge of Vermont flood relief efforts when the flood struck seven months later. Hoover met with Vermont leaders on November 16 to plan for relief and reconstruction. Eight thousand Vermonters were given food, clothing, shelter, and medical assistance. A Vermont flood credit corporation was formed, awarding low-interest loans to businesses, merchants, and farmers who needed them. From federal assistance came money to rebuild bridges, dams, and roads.

With the knowledge that protecting forests in the state would help prevent floods in the future, Vermont proposed 300,000 acres for a national forest. In 1932 the 102,000-acre Green Mountain Forest was proclaimed. Seven years later an additional 160,000 acres were set aside. In 2007 Vermont's National Forest numbered 385,000 acres. In this way, the 1927 flood was responsible for reshaping the state's material, political, and social environment. For more information on the Vermont Flood of 1927, see: www.vpr.net/episode/42038; www.northlandjournal.com/stories19.html; www.vuhs.org/project/water.htm

Photo courtesy Vermont Historical Society

Twenty-eight lives were lost in Bolton, near Camel's Hump, in the 1927 flood. Here a man rows away from a Bolton house on the south bank of the Winooski River.

# 2

## Southeast

**It's called "Banana** *Belt East" by Vermonters living to the north, largely because the snow usually disappears as early as May 1, and consecutive days below zero seldom reach double digits. But there are nonmeteorological attributes to be highlighted as well. Paul Simon's percussionist has his drums made here. One of the towns was named for its surveyor, who—in establishing original boundaries—walked backward into the river that bears his name and drowned.*

*What else . . . Rudyard Kipling wrote some of his best work in Dummerston, before he was driven out of the country. Oh yes, you'll find out why. And one of our nation's richest woman ever (richer even than Oprah Winfrey) became known more for her ability to pinch pennies than as the Wall Street tycoon she became. She was so cheap, in fact, that she relied solely on free health clinics to treat her son for a leg infection that ultimately resulted in an amputation. And speaking of being careful with your pennies, only a U.S. senator from Vermont could have conducted his entire election campaign for a total cost of $1.08. That would be George Aiken.*

*By the way, you probably didn't know you could get some of the best barbecue in the country here, did you? This isn't idle hype; Gourmet magazine says so. It's all here, folks.*

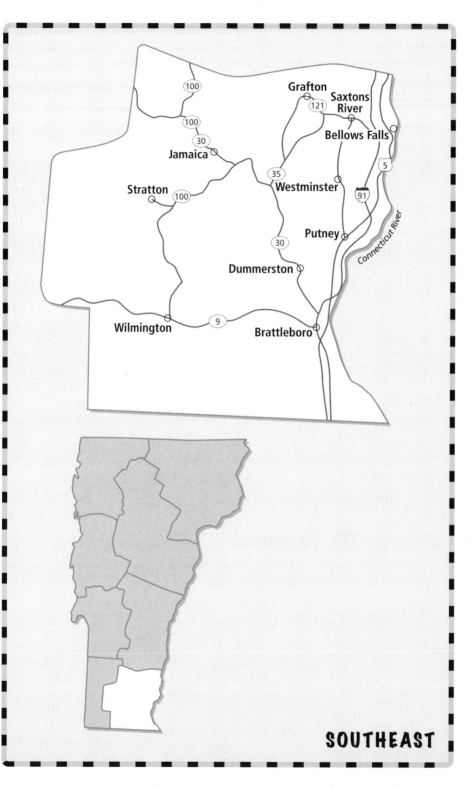

SOUTHEAST

★ ★ ★ ★ ★ ★ ★ ★ ★ ★ ★ ★ ★ ★ ★ ★ ★ ★ ★ ★ ★ ★ ★ ★ ★ ★ ★ ★

## What's a Petroglyph, You Ask?

Bellows Falls

Walking east for about 30 feet on the south side of Bellows Falls'
Vilas Bridge, you'll see, just above the waterline, two fading yellow
paint stripes about 10 feet apart, each indicating the location of eight
to twelve faces carved into the rock. Depending on which researcher
you talk to they are thought to be prehistoric Indian carvings 2,000
or more years old, or only 300 years old but possibly commemorating a battle with settlers in the early 1700s. The dating was made
difficult by the good intentions of the local chapter of the Daughters
of the Revolution who decided to deepen the carvings to make them
more visible. No comment.

Spotting the petroglyphs often is not easy. The view from Vilas
Bridge is preferable to following the sign on the north side of Bridge
Street, which directs viewers down an abandoned railroad spur on
the south side of the street. There is no follow-up information as to
how far down the road the carvings can be seen nor, except for a
yellow paint splotch on a post-and-cable guardrail, any marking that
would point one in the right direction. An opening near the guardrail hints at the existence of a treacherous path down the embank-
ment, which probably shouldn't be attempted unless by rappelling.
Needless to say, wearing high heels or sandals could be hazardous
to your health.

Directions: If you are driving north on U.S. Route 5, turn right on
Westminster Street, and right again 2 blocks farther on Bridge Street.
Park in one of the spaces in front of the Bellows Falls Post Office. Or
drive east another 100 yards, turning right into the abandoned railroad spur opposite the indian carvings sign. Note: The carvings are
often underwater during spring runoff in March and April.

## A Relic in Its Own Right

Bellows Falls

The Miss Bellows Falls Diner, built in the late 1920s by the Worcester Lunch Car Company, is Vermont's only surviving barrel-roofed diner. The restaurant, moved to Bellows Falls from Massachusetts in 1942, features porcelain panels and railroad-style windows on its exterior and its original marble counter, tile floor, and oak and chrome highlights.

Directions: Miss Bellows Falls Diner is on Westminster Street. Going north, it's on the left 1 block beyond the clock tower. (Breakfast is excellent. I hear lunch isn't bad, either.) For more information visit the Web site at www.missbellowsfallsdiner.com.

Photo courtesy of the author

Listed in the National Registry of Historic Places, the Miss Bellows Falls Diner in a former life was called Frankie and Johnny's.

★ ★ ★ ★ ★ ★ ★ ★ ★ ★ ★ ★ ★ ★ ★ ★ ★ ★ ★ ★ ★ ★ ★ ★ ★ ★ ★ ★ ★ ★ ★ ★ ★ ★

### Hetty Green, Richest Woman in the World
Bellows Falls

Adjusted for twenty-first-century dollars, Hetty Green is the richest American woman in history. Her fortune when she died in 1916 was estimated at $100 million, which in today's dollars is more than $2.5 billion—more than Oprah Winfrey, who made the latest top-twenty list. Yet she is remembered more for her eccentricities than for her millions.

Hetty Howland Robinson was born in New Bedford, Massachusetts, in 1834. Her father and grandfather were millionaire owners of a large whaling fleet. At age six she could read the day's financial papers; at eight she opened her first savings account. When her father died, he left Hetty $7.5 million, much of which she invested in railroads and real estate.

Hetty Green's tough negotiating tactics earned her the nickname "Witch of Wall Street." They also made her the richest woman in the world.

Photo courtesy Vermont Historical Society

In her early thirties Hetty met and married Edward Green, a wealthy silk and tea trader who had spent twenty years in the Orient. They had two children, Ned and Sylvia, and moved to Edward's family home in Bellows Falls. Hetty did not change the penny-pinching ways she developed as a child: She walked blocks to buy broken cookies in bulk, returned her berry boxes for a nickel, carried a small can to get the best price on milk for her cat, and once spent hours looking for a

two-cent stamp. Though most of her eccentric behavior was viewed
as harmless, she once refused to pay a doctor to treat Ned's knee,
dislocated in a sledding accident with the damage exacerbated a year
later when he was hit by a wagon pulled by a Saint Bernard. When
treatment at free clinics failed, Ned's leg was amputated.

Hetty and Edward divorced after Edward's business investments
went sour. When Hetty Green died at age eight-one, she left her
entire estate to her two children. Sylvia gave the rundown Green
family home to the town of Bellows Falls. The site, at the corner
of Westminster and Church Streets, is now occupied by a bank, a
municipal parking lot, and Hetty Green Park.

Directly across School Street from Hetty Green Park (behind the
Banknorth building) is Immanuel Episcopal Church and its adjacent
cemetery at the end of Church Street, where Hetty and other members of her family are buried. Her 8-foot-high obelisk monument is in
the lower cemetery just off the sidewalk, between two tall trees and
halfway from either entrance.

## First Canal in the United States
Bellows Falls

The Erie Canal is perhaps the best known, but the canal system that
realized the dream of mass transportation of goods easily within the
continent began in Vermont. The Erie Canal was opened in 1825
and was called the engineering marvel of the nineteenth century.
But if you go into Bellows Falls, you'll see the plaque that appears
above a bridge over the first canal, designed and built by Samuel
Morey, of Fairlee.

> BELLOWS FALLS CANAL
>
> HERE FIRST CANAL IN UNITED STATES WAS BUILT IN 1802.
> THE BRITISH-OWNED COMPANY WHICH WAS CHARTERED TO
> RENDER THE CONNECTICUT RIVER NAVIGABLE HERE IN 1791
> WAS TEN YEARS BUILDING THE NINE LOCKS AND DAM
> AROUND THE GREAT FALLS, 52-FEET HIGH.

In the early 1800s, boats loaded with lumber and produce avoided the Connecticut River's 52-foot-deep gorge by passing through eight locks on the Bellows Falls Canal.

After the first railroad came through Bellows Falls in 1849, river traffic declined sharply, and the canal has been used ever since for water power only. More than 200 years later, the canal is chugging away, although it is somewhat deeper and wider.

Directions: The Bellows Falls Canal plaque is near the bridge on Bridge Street, 100 yards or so west of the directional sign for the Indian Carvings.

### Oh Boy, What Dari Joy!

Bellows Falls

He didn't know he'd be opening the first soft-serve ice cream stand in Vermont. In 1951 Joseph DeMuzio, a senior at the University of New Hampshire, knew only from his research that this new way of presenting America's favorite treat was going gangbusters on the West Coast, and he wanted in on it.

The budding entrepreneur already had his spot picked out—the empty lot his family owned next to their house. It was a perfect location, facing the Connecticut River and bordered by two main thoroughfares meeting in a V just north of downtown Bellows Falls. Starting with architectural blueprints from a Boston company, he found a contractor in Brattleboro to build it, for $6,000. "Just after he started digging, I went to the local bank for funding," says Joseph. "I was a World War II veteran and knew I was eligible for a G.I. loan."

The drive-in operation first opened its doors in May 1952, with a single soft-serve machine. The name "Dari Joy" came to Joseph in a dream. The rooftop logo you see in the photo he bought from a sign maker in Keene, New Hampshire. It seems he came by one day to say that he had this big old head—from a Bob's Big Boy franchise of another era—in the back of his building, down on the ground and not in the greatest shape. "He said he thought it would look good on the roof and offered to sell it to me," says Joseph.

"In those days the machines were not up to the task of operating consistently, so I had to be a mechanic as well as sell ice cream and hot dogs." From that Spartan menu, over the years Dari Joy has expanded to a full-service restaurant for lunch and dinner, with ten employees. That

Joseph DeMuzio, torn between life as a dentist or an entrepreneur, believes that he made the right choice.

doesn't mean the drive-in has abandoned what got it where it is. In a six-month season, it sells, on average, nearly 2,000 gallons of hard ice cream and more than 5,000 gallons of soft-serve. When Joseph feels he's had enough, he will turn the business over to son Richard. For now though, he enjoys his working life.

Still, running any business has its ins and outs. For example, "a couple of months ago a customer lost control of his car and smashed right through that wall over there," says Joseph, pointing to the spot. "Luckily, no one was hurt. You might say that after fifty-five-plus years, somebody finally drove in." No plaque has been planned to commemorate the point of impact.

Directions: Dari Joy can be reached by going north through the center of Bellows Falls (Rockingham Street), until you come to Green Street near the west bank of the Connecticut River. It is open roughly from mid-April until Columbus Day, 11:00 a.m.–9:00 p.m. weekdays and 11:00 a.m.–10:00 p.m. Saturdays and Sundays.

### Fort Dummer, Vermont's First Nontribal Settlement
Brattleboro

After crossing the Vermont-Massachusetts border from the south on Interstate 91, your first landmark, up on the right, will be the entrance to Fort Dummer State Park. These days, Vermont residents have little need for a fort to protect their turf. Disputes between Vermont and New Hampshire folks, for example, have been largely restricted to complaints by Vermonters that a planned New Hampshire Wal-Mart expansion would be a travesty, in part because it would lead to monumental traffic jams across the border.

Back in the eighteenth century, though, matters were a bit more serious. Fort Dummer was built in 1724 along the banks of the Connecticut River to protect what was then a Massachusetts colony from invasions by the French and Indians. The Salmon Hole Massacre of 1748, for example, was one of hundreds of skirmishes that took place during King George's War, from 1744–1748.

Early one May morning, eighty soldiers led by Captain Eleazer Melvin, of Northfield, Massachusetts, were three weeks into a scouting expedition from Fort Dummer. They stopped at the headwaters of the West River, in Londonderry, believing they had outrun their French and Indian pursuers. Stripping off their packs, they stopped to rest a bit and shoot a few salmon for breakfast. Two French soldiers and nine Indians who had been close behind them heard the shots and quickly located their adversaries. They opened fire from behind logs and trees, killing six soldiers. While killing but six of a group of eighty stretches the definition of *massacre* a bit, you must admit that a confrontation named the "Salmon Hole Massacre" sure has an intriguing ring to it.

Today's park overlooks the site of Fort Dummer, which was flooded when the Vernon Dam was built in 1908. The fort is now underwater, near a lumber company on the Vermont side of the river. The campground, located in the southern foothills of the Green Mountains, includes fifty-one tent/trailer sites and ten lean-to sites along with hot showers but no trailer hookups. Also in the park are a picnic area and hiking trails.

Directions: From I-91, take exit 1. Go 1/10 mile north on U.S. Route 5A, and then go 1/2 mile east on Fairground Road, and finally 1 mile south on Main Street and Old Guilford Road. For more information visit www.vtstateparks.com/htm/fortdummer.cfm.

## The Strolling of the Heifers

Brattleboro

You've heard, perhaps, of the Running of the Bulls, in Pamplona? But what about Brattleboro's annual June "Strolling of the Heifers" festival? During this iconic parade one hundred flower-laden Holstein and Jersey cows—and occasionally a Guernsey or two—make their way down Main Street to a cheering crowd, followed by draft horses, tractors, jugglers, clowns, fire-eaters, and Turkey Hill Dairy employees giving away thousands of cups of ice cream. But it wouldn't be

The 162,000 cows living on Vermont farms are said to produce more than 2.6 billion pounds of milk a year—or more than 16,000 pounds per cow. We'll do the math: That's forty-four pounds per cow per day.

a dairy festival without a milking contest, music by the Heifer Brass Quartet (and at least a dozen other jazz and classical groups), a Dairy Princess Pageant, and a Royal Farmers Feast and Farm Tour. Many festival-goers are sure to be in town the night before the parade, when local farm families are honored for the decades of work they've done to keep southern Vermont's agricultural tradition alive.

So the Strolling of the Heifers not only kicks off National Dairy Month each June but is a way to protect and promote Vermont's agricultural heritage in residents' daily lives. It has raised more than $150,000 for educational programs for more than

Photo courtesy of Jason Henske

The first week each June, "Strolling of the Heifers" kicks off National Dairy Month as a salute to family farms and their many contributions to Vermont's agricultural heritage.

eighty schools in Windham County, including a scholarship program that will fund farmers and agricultural students.

For more information visit the event's official Web site: www .strollingoftheheifers.com.

## The First Ever U.S. Stamp?

Brattleboro

According to *The Annals of Brattleboro, 1681–1895*, Frederick Palmer, a young music teacher from Maine, moved to Brattleboro in 1836 to seek a better life. He did just that by marrying a young lady whose father was partner in a prestigious law firm. A few years later, Frederick caught the attention of President James K. Polk, to the extent that in 1845 he was appointed postmaster of Brattleboro.

In those days postmasters were paid solely on daily receipts, so this induced Palmer to use a good deal of his spare time thinking up ideas that would supplement the family income. Just a year later, in 1846, he came up with the Brattleboro Stamp, which he asked Springfield engraver Thomas Chubbuck to design. (Considering that the Brattleboro Post Office had revenues of just $1,700 in 1847, the $9 Dr. Palmer paid for engraving and printing his stamps was a relatively large out-of-pocket expense.)

Palmer's first-year sales were encouraging, but on July 1, 1847, unfortunately, Congress passed legislation, the Post Office Act, allowing for the creation of national, prepaid stamps. This resulted in the balance of the original issue of 500 (or 5,000, accounts vary) Brattleboro Stamps being destroyed. In its place, by the time Congress got its act together, the five-cent Franklin and the ten-cent Washington appeared—serviceable enough, but they were no Brattleboros, to be sure. This automatically downgraded the Brattleboro Stamp to "provisional" status, meaning that it was invalid for use in any post office other than the one in which it was issued. This technicality has resulted in its losing its "First U.S. Stamp" status.

★ ★ ★ ★ ★ ★ ★ ★ ★ ★ ★ ★ ★ ★ ★ ★ ★ ★ ★ ★ ★ ★ ★ ★ ★ ★ ★

Nevertheless, some 160 or so years later the Brattleboro—the first known U.S. stamp to be adhesive, by the way—is still a philatelic hot ticket. If you come across one in good condition, it can fetch as much as $110,000, according to the Stamp Auction Network. Keep your eyes open!

## Brattleboro, Home of Art Deco

Brattleboro

The Latchis Hotel and Theatre is one of only two Art Deco buildings in the state of Vermont. When the movie house was built in 1938, it was the centerpiece of a fourteen-theater complex throughout New England created by Peter Latchis and his Greek immigrant father, Demetrius, who sold fruit from a pushcart as his first job in the United States.

The theatre portion of the Latchis Hotel and Theatre was designed in a Greek mythology theme. Its "Hollywood, Dine and Recline" package includes a movie pass, dinner, and one night's lodgings.

✦ ✦ ✦ ✦ ✦ ✦ ✦ ✦ ✦ ✦ ✦ ✦ ✦ ✦ ✦ ✦ ✦ ✦ ✦ ✦ ✦ ✦ ✦ ✦ ✦ ✦ ✦ ✦ ✦ ✦

In 2003 the Brattleboro Arts Initiative joined in buying the building from the Latchis family to restore the theater and hotel to create a first-rate center for the arts in downtown Brattleboro.

The main theater—there are also two smaller screening rooms, with another one yet planned—is dominated by Doric-columned facades of Greek temple replicas on both sides of the room. The ceiling is a light blue, bedecked with sparkling stars and the twelve signs of the zodiac. Continuing the art nouveau interior is a tableau of the lovable Leto and her infants, Apollo and Artemis.

Directions: To reach the Latchis Hotel and Theatre, at 50 Main Street, from I-91, use exit 2 and take Route 9 east toward town. Follow Route 9 as it becomes Western Avenue and then High Street, until it intersects Main. Take a right and go 2 blocks to the corner of Flat Street. For more information on the hotels and great vacation packages, visit www.latchis.com, or call (800) 798-6301.

## Indian British Yankee Go Home!

Dummerston

In 1892, at the age of twenty-seven, poet and novelist Rudyard Kipling married an American girl and moved from London to Dummerston, Vermont, just north of Brattleboro. Kipling already was internationally famous when he married Caroline Balestier, whose recently deceased brother had been Kipling's good friend. The couple built a grand house with a distant view of New Hampshire's Mount Monadnock, near Carrie's parents' home. Kipling, who was a British subject born in India, named his new home Naulakha, Indian for "precious jewel."

In just a few months, Kipling began receiving more mail in Dummerston than the largest business in nearby Brattleboro. U.S. Postmaster General Wilson authorized a special post office (to this day, it is said, the only one ever created for an individual) to handle the author's letters and packages. "Waite, Vermont" was located in the home of Kipling's neighbor, Anna Waite, who was also appointed

★ ★ ★ ★ ★ ★ ★ ★ ★ ★ ★ ★ ★ ★ ★ ★ ★ ★ ★ ★ ★ ★ ★ ★ ★ ★ ★ ★ ★ ★ ★

Rudyard Kipling named his house in Vermont "Naulakha," from the title of a book he wrote with American friend Wolcott Balestier—whose sister he later married.

postmaster. The Waite postmark has been prized by philatelists for more than a century.

Kipling loved his time in Vermont, and at Naulakha over the next four years, he wrote the *Jungle Book* and *Captains Courageous* and began work on *Kim* and the *Just So Stories*. Compared to his calloused, hardworking farmer neighbors, however, Kipling was thought to be a man who "didn't work," and who spent inordinate amounts of time playing with his two little girls, Josephine and Elsie. (In his spare time he also designed what is believed to be the first tennis court in Vermont and painted golf balls red to "invent" winter golf.)

Eventually, Kipling's dream life became a nightmare. Carrie had a serious falling-out with her other brother, Beatty, who was described variously as a "feckless alcoholic" and unmatched in "sheer boorishness." A lurid lawsuit, trial, and much negative publicity followed the muscular Beatty's threat to "kick the god-damned soul" out of the much smaller and slightly built Kipling. After four years in America, total withdrawal seemed the only way out, so the Kipling family returned to England.

Back home Kipling told his friends: "There are only two places in the world where I want to live—Bombay and Brattleboro. And I can't live in either."

Naulakha was the Landmark Trust's first property in North America, which means you and up to seven other Kipling fans can rent it and stay where the great author himself once lived. Up to eight guests may stay at Naulakha, which includes four bedrooms (three twin, one double); three bathrooms; full kitchen; washer, dryer and dishwasher. Dogs are allowed. All bookings must be made through the Office of the Landmark Trust in England: Shottesbrooke, Maidenhead, Berkshire SL6 3SW, United Kingdom, tel. 011 44 1628 825925; fax. 011 44 1628 825417.

Directions: The Kipling home is located north of Brattleboro, off I-91 at exit 3. Turn south on U.S. Route 5 at the traffic circle, right on Black Mountain Road, and right again to 707 Kipling Road. Visit www.landmarktrustusa.org/naulakha/index.html for more information about renting Naulakha and also about the history and renovation of the home.

### They Don't Make Senators like George Anymore

Dummerston

George D. Aiken, born in Dummerston and educated in Putney and Brattleboro, was a maverick Republican Vermont U.S. senator for thirty-four years, from 1941 to 1975 and Vermont's governor for one term before that. Senator Mike Mansfield, a Democratic leader in the Senate during the time Aiken served, called him "the wise old owl" for his statement during the Vietnam War that we should declare victory and get out—a balance between the "hawks" who wanted victory and the "doves" who wanted to withdraw at any cost.

Aiken wrote of a "Vermont with a heritage of ideals that included the principles of loving liberty, self-reliance, thrift, and liberalism." The senator practiced what he preached. As to thrift and self-reliance alone, in his last campaign for office at age seventy-five, he spent only $17. And this was only his second least expensive campaign. In 1956 he was able to get by on $1.08. If, as they say, money buys access, Senator George Aiken got significantly more than his money's worth, as did his constituents.

### Percussion Instruments to the Stars
Gageville (North Westminster)

Driving west on Route 121, about a mile out of Bellows Falls, you'll see a small sawmill on the left. From the outside the long, low build- ings, stacks of lumber, forklifts, and cones of sawdust will remind you of most sawmills you've seen in your lifetime: men using machines to convert felled trees into planks, timbers, and milled wood pieces of various sizes and shapes.

But Cooperman is one of the last of what used to be known as "fife and drum companies." It still manufactures both drums and fifes—four models of rope-tension field drums and a dozen variet- ies of fifes alone. But it also produces what no other company in the world does: hundreds of bodhráns, tars, bendirs, hadjiras, ghavals, kanjiras, riqs, and pandeiros. "Huh?" you say. These happen to be custom-made hand drums that originated in North Africa, Morocco, India, Egypt, Persia, and Azerbaijan—all in high demand by percus- sionists and hand drummers throughout the jazz, folk, classical, and contemporary music worlds. (Paul Simon's percussionist Jamey Haddad designed the Cooperman hadjira, which actually is a twen- tieth-century adaptation of several existing drums from Egypt, Brazil, and south India.)

"The drumheads are made from calfskin and goatskin—in the case of the riqs, from fish skin," says Patrick Cooperman, who heads the company. "The tannery for our only domestic head producer, in

Sheboygan, Wisconsin, just burned down. Now we rely on tanneries in England, Germany, and Pakistan. Each has its own distinctive sound for different instruments."

"My father began building drums more than forty years ago," says Patrick, "and started the company with my mother, who still works here." Actually, five members of the Cooperman family are employed by the company, which numbers just twenty-one men and women.

The 2,000–2,500 hardwood logs Cooperman goes through each year also result in sixty finished banjos and one hundred tambourines weekly. "We use only the butt log," says Patrick, "which is the first

Master drum-maker (and vice president) Jim Ellis puts the finishing touches on a rope tension post-Civil War-style field drum at the Cooperman Fife and Drum Company.

eight feet of the tree." The trees are all local hardwoods: poplar, cherry, ash, maple, and birch.

Every other wooden-instrument manufacturer has gone to laminated wood, but Cooperman alone forms its drum and string-instrument frames from wood bent by machine after it is steamed to optimum flexibility.

Does Paul Simon know his percussionist buys custom-made instruments from a little sawmill in rural Vermont? "If you asked him that question, I think he'd be dumbfounded," Patrick says.

Directions: For more information see www.cooperman.com or call (802) 463-9750.

## Grafton's Record-Setting Postmasters
Grafton

*Albert Neill, an area resident with ancestral roots in Grafton, supplies this recollection:*

"Cousin Fannie Hall was postmaster of the village of Grafton from the age of sixteen until the day she died, in her sixties. Her mother was postmaster before her. She took over for Fannie's dad, who died after a year on the job. Together with her mother and father, the three hold a national record—I'm told—of seventy years for consecutive family postmaster tenure. Cousin Fannie lived next door, just beyond the post office in a beautiful big brick home, with the archway above. I think it's a vacation rental now, called Eaglebrook. At one time the top floor of that dwelling was a dance hall and tavern, but that was her home. She had no electricity; she had a hand pump in the kitchen and an outhouse in the woodshed.

"One time, the story goes, she had a visitor up from the city. He had heard that if you put a felt hat on the rim of the seat in an outhouse, it would keep your butt warm. So he decided to take that approach. But he forgot one thing: He forgot to cut the crown out of the hat.

Homes on Houghtonville Road, just a block north of Cousin Fannie's post office, in Grafton.

"Another story was that the townspeople were so beholden to Fannie for her service that they decided to give her electricity. They took up a collection to install it, and she promptly gave the money to charity. So they raised the money again—and this time they hired an electrician, who went in and wired the house. Actually this was a good thing, because in her latter years she loved to sit on her couch with her cat and listen to the radio.

"When cousin Fannie died, she left the post office to me. So I owned the post office when I was in college. But a prominent state senator lived in Grafton at the time. He said to my father, 'You know, the historical society needs a home.' So my dad gave *my* post office to the historical society!"

★ ★ ★ ★ ★ ★ ★ ★ ★ ★ ★ ★ ★ ★ ★ ★ ★ ★ ★ ★ ★ ★ ★ ★ ★ ★

Directions: From Saxtons River, drive east on Route 121 for 7 miles. The red, one-story frame building just over the bridge on the right, just beyond the old firehouse, is the former post office, now a real estate agency. (The Historical Society found a new home just up the block.) The red brick building just beyond is Fannie Hall's former home.

## Vixen and Friend

Jamaica

Warren Patrick spends part of each day working on his memoirs. He's got a lot to say: 97 years of travel and just plain living to get down on paper. He's raised three daughters and worked as a farmer and an aircraft engine worker during World War II. He also had a real estate business.

Since his wife died in 1994. Warren has been pretty much on his own. In the summer there's the lawn to cut, and he works out regularly lifting weights. "No, I don't miss a day," he says. Exercise is what keeps me going."

Photo courtesy of Joyce Pelos

**Warren Patrick waits for Vixen to get close enough to feed.**

As an amateur photographer, Warren has learned to closely observe the world around him. This is what helped him spot a fox limping on a game forepaw toward the back of his property in 2005. Winter was coming, and Warren began to leave food for the visitor he named Vixen. Every morning at 8:30 Vixen arrived for breakfast. Some mornings she would arrive early and nap on Warren's porch couch until he put the food out. When she was late, Warren would call her.

Over time Vixen's leg improved, and two springs later Warren noticed four kits with her, lurking on the edge of the woods—unseen, so they thought. For several months, Vixen and Warren maintained their routine, until the day a neighbor reported a fox dead on Route 100, near his house. When Vixen failed to show up the following week, Warren knew his friend was gone.

Now he's concerned about the kits. They're more timid than Vixen was. He's seen only two of them; so he's not sure if all are still alive, or if he's seeing the same two And it turns out they're nocturnal: Instead of appearing at 8:30 a.m. as their mother did, he sees them at 8:30 p.m.

"About a half-hour ago," Warren wrote in an e-mail message to one of his daughters recently, "I was watching for a fox to come. A raccoon showed up and started eating the dog food. A bit later a fox arrived and watched the coon for a couple of minutes. Then the fox came over and they both started eating. At one point they were only a foot apart, with no sign of either 'fear or fight.' I had two cameras but it was just too dark to get a picture. What a sight! Dad."

Warren is sure the "Vixen and Family" chapter of his memoirs is going to be special.

## Taste Delights from a School Bus in a Meadow
Putney

If you drive into Curtis's Barbecue most any day between 10:00 a.m. and dusk, look to the right. You'll see smoke curling above a meat pit as rows of rising gray beams meet the sunshine. Right away you

★ ★ ★ ★ ★ ★ ★ ★ ★ ★ ★ ★ ★ ★ ★ ★ ★ ★ ★ ★ ★ ★ ★ ★ ★ ★ ★ ★ ★

know something special is afoot. The entrance sign reads: NINTH WON-
DER OF THE WORLD. That sounds about right.

With a long-handled fork, Curtis Tuff deftly moves five-pound
slabs of pork ribs and half chickens to warmer or cooler spots on
his 5-foot-by-10-foot grill, depending on their degree of doneness.
Sleeping soundly next to that grill is C.J. (Curtis Jr.), his pet pig—
never, he swears, to be on the menu. Behind Curtis in this three-
acre meadow are two blue school buses where orders are filled,
including side dishes such as baked potatoes, coleslaw, corn on the
cob, and baked beans. Says *Gourmet* magazine's roadside reporter
Michael Stern: "The ribs are cooked so the meat pulls off in big, suc-
culent strips that virtually burst with piggy flavor and the perfume of
smoke." Both spicy and mild homemade sauces are at the ready.

Just out of sight beyond the bus (right) is the grill tended by Curtis,
where seven days a week, seven months a year, he works to justify his
"Ninth Wonder of the World" renown.

★ ★ ★ ★ ★ ★ ★ ★ ★ ★ ★ ★ ★ ★ ★ ★ ★ ★ ★ ★ ★ ★ ★ ★ ★ ★ ★ ★ ★ ★

In a state better known for cheese and maple syrup, ribs are about the last specialty food you'd expect to find. Yet Curtis has been at this site since 1968, going through twenty-one cords of hardwood or more every season (at least five of which he splits himself). He has put two daughters through Vermont Academy and Mount Ida College, one of whom, with her husband, recently opened a branch of Curtis's Barbecue in Chester, Vermont.

Directions: From I-91, take exit 4 and go north on U.S. Route 5 for less than half a mile. Curtis's Barbecue is on the right, just before the service station. Curtis's is open April through October, Thursday–Sunday, 10:00 a.m. to dusk. For more information visit www.curtisbqvt.com or call (802) 387-5474.

## Last Dairy Farm in Rockingham
Rockingham Township

Twice a day, 365 days a year, Arnold Fisher's fifty-five cows—fifty-four Holsteins and a Jersey—cross Pleasant Valley Road. Orange caution cones slow down drivers who otherwise would not know to brake at the top of the hill and around the blind curve approaching the Fisher farm. Each morning after milking, the cows move out to pasture, spending the day grazing and resting. At about 3:00 p.m. they come back for the evening milking and feeding.

"When I moved here in 1950, there were a little more than fifty dairy farms in the township," says Arnold Fisher. "Today there's just me."

"Did he tell you he drove those cows over here from Fisher Hill, in Grafton [about an 8-mile drive]?" fellow farmer and neighbor Dick Stickney asks me a day after my conversation with Arnold. Fisher Hill was settled by Fishers a couple hundred years ago, and Arnold is descended from them. I ask Arnold how he has managed to be the only one left standing. "One thing that has helped is that people come up from Connecticut or New York to buy property, but they don't want to farm. They want a piece of Vermont. So that's made land available for us to use at a reasonable price. We don't cut any

★ ★ ★ ★ ★ ★ ★ ★ ★ ★ ★ ★ ★ ★ ★ ★ ★ ★ ★ ★ ★ ★ ★ ★ ★ ★ ★ ★ ★ ★ ★ ★ ★ ★

hay here at home, but we cut about 12,000 bales on other fields, as well as fifty acres of corn for silage on fields 3 to 10 miles away."

This last year has been one of the worst for Fisher and dairy farmers in general. "A year ago there was a surplus of milk, so the price was way down. Now the price is up, because there's a shortage of milk. I think somebody knows the reason behind it, but I don't." The cost of machinery, fuel, and other expenses are so high that it's hard to keep going. The bigger farms get help, but that help doesn't seem to trickle down to the family farmer. Organic farming has been the answer for some. The cost is higher, but so is the return.

Looking forward to its milking after a hard day's grazing, Arnold Fisher's herd heads home across Pleasant Valley Road, in Rockingham.

The Fisher farm is an owner-member of the Cabot/Agri-Mark Cooperative. Every other day a gleaming silver tank truck with the Cabot logo stops at the barn to pick up the 3,000 pounds of milk produced by Fisher cows.

"Yes," says Dick Stickney, "since the days Arnold and I went to high school in Bellows Falls in the forties, we've owned equipment

★ ★ ★ ★ ★ ★ ★ ★ ★ ★ ★ ★ ★ ★ ★ ★ ★ ★ ★ ★ ★ ★ ★ ★ ★ ★ ★ ★ ★

together, double-dated, gone to Red Sox games, and made maple syrup together. I gave up dairy farming ten years ago when my son left to become farm manager at Putney School. Now there's just Arnold."

Poet Ogden Nash once reduced the entire dairy farming industry to a mere couplet:

*The cow is of the bovine ilk;*
*One end is moo, the other milk.*

True as far as it goes, but Arnold Fisher and Dick Stickney will tell you there's a lot more involved getting from the moo to the milk.

Directions: Both the Fisher and Stickney farms are just beyond Saxtons River on Pleasant Valley Road, which runs between Routes 121 and 103. From Route 121, Dick Stickney's farm is about 2.5 miles north. Arnold Fisher's farm is less than a mile beyond that.

### An Uncommonly Fatal Survey?

Saxtons River

Each year the organizers of Saxtons River's Fourth of July festivities prepare a program that includes the day's happenings, as well as a short history of the village. The program is available to everyone waiting to watch the traditional parade. *Traditional* in this sense means quality valued over quantity. In years past, for example, the relatively small procession ran through town west to east, and then made a return pass from east to west. The program I read included the information that Saxtons River—municipality as well as river—both were named for surveyor Frederick Saxton. Unfortunately, Mr. Saxton never experienced the glory this fact should have afforded him. While fixing the boundary between Westminster and Rockingham Townships, the unfortunate surveyor fell into the river and drowned.

But wait! A look at the 1859 *Gazetteer of Vermont* tells us that "a Mr. Saxton . . . unluckily fell in while crossing [the river] on a log . . . but was not drowned." And, writes Dr. Silvio Bedini in a May–June 2004 *American Surveyor* story, "that particular surveyor named Saxton has not

been identified." Dr. Bedini determined that actually there were at least two surveyors named Frederick Saxton—father and son, it is presumed—and that both of them were reported to have drowned, "but neither was the Saxton for whom the river may have been named."

Hmm.

As early as 1724, and before any surveys in the area had been made, the river already was known as "Saxtons River." So might there have been a *third* Saxton, perhaps also named Frederick? And might he also have been a surveyor? This, writes Dr. Bedini, is the sole remaining mystery unsolved.

Enough conjecture. It was time to consult someone in a position to provide more light than heat. I called on Louise Thompson, born in Saxtons River 102 years ago on April 23. Ms. Thompson, a psychiatric social worker for more than fifty years and a graduate of both Middlebury and Smith Colleges, and daughter of the owner of a local hardware store and lumber mill for several decades in the nineteenth century, was a reasonable choice. A charming lady who reads avidly and completes at least one crossword puzzle a day, Ms. Thompson, who does not look her age, has a full head of snow white hair combed back from her lightly lined face. On the day we met she wore a green cardigan, white blouse, and khaki pants and was accompanied by Jean Anderson, one of three rotating nurse/companions.

We talked for a while before I mentioned to her what I had learned so far. "You know all the stories, I'm sure," I said.

"Well, some of them, anyway," she agreed.

"Do you have any idea which one is true?" I asked.

Louise paused a moment. "Not in the slightest," she said.

And there we have it.

## L. L. B. Angas—"The Major"
Saxtons River

On April 9, 1935, New York newspaper financial pages ran the following boxed ad: "Major Lawrence Lee Bazley Angas, Investment

Counsel, has taken an office at the Waldorf-Astoria. He respectfully solicits inquiries." This marked the arrival from England of a dashing, flamboyant, mustachioed Oxford University graduate who was a Wall Street force to be reckoned with for the next twenty years, and who for almost twenty years thereafter ran one of the most bizarre one-man entrepreneurial empires ever seen in Saxtons River, Vermont. Major Angas was drawn to the United States in the depths of the American Depression after writing a successful pamphlet for Simon & Schuster called *The Coming of the American Boom.* His accurate predictions earned him such clients as J.P. Morgan & Co. and the United States Treasury. (His $200/hour consultation fee, converted from 1940 dollars, would be $2,500 today, and allowed him to care adequately for the wife and daughter he left in England.) The Major wore his rapidly accelerating wealth with style. He drove 12-cylinder

The former residence of financier Lawrence Lee Bazley Angas.

★ ★ ★ ★ ★ ★ ★ ★ ★ ★ ★ ★ ★ ★ ★ ★ ★ ★ ★ ★ ★ ★ ★ ★ ★ ★ ★ ★

Cadillac convertibles. His custom-tailored suits included inside pouch pockets for emergency quantities of 12-inch Havana cigars and copies of his *Angas Digests*. The refrigerator he installed in his Waldorf-Astoria suite always held enough champagne, hors d'oeuvres, gin, and vermouth to stock the impromptu parties he frequently hosted.

Saxtons River resident Humphrey Neill, another Wall Street guru during Angas's New York years, was destined to meet him and become friends because their personalities meshed so well. Neill was as much of an iconoclast as was the Major, and in 1954 convinced him to move to Saxtons River and leave the city's hustle and bustle to carry out his work in a quieter, more peaceful atmosphere.

Unfortunately, Major Angas brought more of his bombastic personality to Saxtons River than any peace and quiet he took from the community. An avid and excellent golfer, he often drove balls down the middle of Pleasant Street outside the first house he bought in the village—at midnight or later, in his underwear, after a hard day of writing. When confronted by a neighbor the morning after one such occasion, he said in shocked surprise: "You must be mistaken. What was I wearing?" When she reminded him, he replied: "You know, it's not proper for a young woman to spy on an old man."

After two years, the Major bought the Saxtons River Inn on Main Street—with its five-story tower, the largest building in town—and turned it into his personal home and office. All twenty-five of the guest rooms became receptacles for his growing quantities of books and files. The few friends and neighbors who were invited to visit for canned salmon and champagne said that even the large dining room and adjacent parlor were crammed with boxes, crowded shelves, and bookcases to the extent that it was almost impossible to navigate from room to room. A two-story side porch running the length of the inn was converted to a driving range—complete with a net to practice his swing—because the Major was writing the ultimate book on golf. He became even more reclusive, but did find space in his

Cadillac-strewn parking lot to create an ice rink for town youngsters. (He was also a first-rate skater and skier, and competed for England in the 1912 Olympics.)

The Major's death in 1973, two days before his 80th birthday, was as dramatic as his life had been. Late one evening, it is thought while in his third-floor bedroom warming himself in front of an electric heater, his bathrobe caught fire. He ran down the two flights of stairs and rolled in the snow to put out the blaze, but his burns were so severe that he died after being taken to Bellows Falls Hospital. He is buried across the river in the town cemetery, next to his friend Humphrey Neill.

The Inn at Saxtons River, as it is now called, is easy to spot on Main Street in the center of town. The Saxtons River Cemetery is across the bridge, where both the Major and Humphrey Neill are buried, one block up the hill and on the left. See the "Grave Location Directory" just outside the cemetery. Humphrey Neill's house, still in the family, is three blocks west of the Inn on Pleasant Valley Road, on the right just after Route 121 curves left. Visit www.innsaxtonsriver.com.

### Tim Clark, Minimalist Sugar Producer

Saxtons River

We'll let Tim tell this story himself.

"One Saturday morning in March 2006, I was awakened by daughters Anna and Lia's cadenced cries: 'No maple syrup! No maple syrup!' As I drove to the market, I vowed this would never happen again. And from this small dilemma, a maple-sugaring business was born.

"As founder, research and development fell to me. Then fate stepped in. Dave Moore, a local inn owner and paint contractor, pulled into our driveway with his two sons and a few dozen empty tin buckets in his pickup bed later that morning. Hearing my plan, Dave looked me straight in the eye. 'Four words,' he said. 'Tree selection is key.' We narrowed our search to the only sugar maple on our

property. Its girth suggested to Dave that we had a three- or four-bucket specimen. I opted modestly for the three-bucket option. Our one-family, one-tree business could always expand.

"Over the next few days we assembled pots, pans, filter paper, candy thermometer, and jars from our kitchen, cellar, and the local general store: Then came the sap collection. We boiled it on the kitchen stove to evaporate the water; sampled and quality controlled the resulting syrup; and, finally, bottled and marketed our product. Along the way we learned about the sap-bucket drip rate, bug and debris filtration, and fuel-to-boiling-temperature ratio. These are among the technical issues that assaulted us those first few days.

"All start-up manufacturing ventures face critical viability moments. Either make the right call or fail. Our moment came when I noticed

Vermont sugar maker Tim Clark adjusts the window display of his season's syrup batch. Technical innovations he has undertaken are expected to triple next year's production.

Photo courtesy Tim Clark

that using our soup pot to turn sap into syrup was going to take forever. Instead, I bought a large, shallow aluminum pan that covered two stove burners. We tripled our boil-time efficiency with that one move alone. At the end of the first week, we were enjoying our first home-made maple syrup.

"Looking back at that first 2006 production run, it seems amazing that we were able to produce anything remotely resembling syrup with our crude technology. The next season our technique and efficiency improved. Not only did we meet our family syrup needs, but neighbors and friends benefited as well. With new maple saplings sprouting in our backyard, we believe sweet success seems likely for generations to come."

## Stratton Mountain: World Headquarters for Snowboarding
Stratton Village

The "first snowboard-like" device, a plank of plywood and a length of clothesline, is said to have been invented by M. J. "Jack" Burchett in 1929. The dozens of references to Jack on the hundreds of Web sites devoted to the topic are remarkably similar in wording, yet not one mentions anything else about Jack's life or identifies his home-town, state, or country of origin. Was the first of these writers simply inventing an event to give the sport more panache and a longer timeline? If so, the dozens of snowboard "historians" trailing behind need to get a life. And even so, "a plank of plywood and a length of clothesline"? At best, "Jack" appears to be someone who really wanted to toboggan standing up but couldn't afford a toboggan. We are outraged.

Most people agree that the sport of snowboarding began in the eastern half of the United States, specifically in Vermont. There are claims from the Mount Baker area of Washington, and even from Breckenridge, Massachusetts, but Stratton Mountain near Bondville gets most of the votes. Stratton Mountain has been home to the U.S. Open Snowboarding Championships for more than twenty years and opened its lifts and trails to snowboarding in 1983.

★ ★ ★ ★ ★ ★ ★ ★ ★ ★ ★ ★ ★ ★ ★ ★ ★ ★ ★ ★ ★ ★ ★ ★ ★ ★ ★ ★

When snowboarding pioneer Bud Keene was asked by *Vermont Sports Online* why Vermont has produced so many outstanding snow-boarders, he said: "There are more halfpipes along Route 100 than in most other places in the U.S. And then there's the eastern mindset—riding in bad weather, in adverse conditions, riding on ice. . . . Tradition also plays a role. This is the birth of snowboarding and it makes for a small ecosystem back here."

Stratton Mountain Resort is located on the highest peak in southern Vermont, 20 miles from Manchester. It is the largest resort in the region. If you visit, a twelve-passenger gondola will take you from the resort to the peak of 3,936-foot Stratton Mountain.

Directions: From 1-91, take exit 2, and then on Route 30 drive approximately 30 miles north to Bondville. Stratton Mountain Resort is 4 miles from Bondville. For more information visit www.stratton .com, which tells not only about the resort but also about the surrounding area, or call (800) 787-2886.

### Ice-Fishing Central

Wilmington

As long as there's been a Vermont, there's been ice fishing. Actually, if the number of queries e-mailed to the Ice Fishing Chat Forum is to be believed, Michigan and Vermont attract the most North American icefishianados, followed closely by Maine.

Though most anglers store their fishing gear for the winter, more and more start cutting holes in the ice as soon as it's safe to walk on a lake, a pond, a reservoir, or parts of some rivers. Every February for the past twenty-five years, for example, the Deerfield Valley Sports-men's Club has sponsored the Harriman Reservoir Ice Fishing Derby, one of dozens around the state.

The first time they put this derby together, in 1985, it attracted 223 fishermen, fisherwomen, and fisherkids These days the event averages more than 800 participants and stretches over two days. In addition to Harriman's ample fish population, the reservoir is stocked each year with 150 tagged brook, rainbow, and brown trout, plus a slew of perch and small- and large-mouth bass.

Catching the most-wanted tagged fish entitles the lucky angler to a $25,000 pickup truck. Total cash prizes average more than $60,000, including a $10,000 first prize. The largest nontagged trout and bass also are awarded trophies and small cash prizes as well, in a number of categories.

Families set up shanties, particularly those who fish continuously over the two-day period. Those not barbecuing moose, bear, or other delicacies can buy snacks and baked goodies at stands run by high school students.

"We start soliciting the big sponsors in June," says derby organizer Debra Cox, "because if you wait any later, they don't have any advertising money left when it's time to put on the derby. We print 15,000 papers distributed all over the state, plus in New Hampshire, Massachusetts, and New York."

It could have been one of these papers that reached three young men in Massachusetts, who one year sent in registration fees and arrived at the Harriman with a few 36-inch farm-raised salmon in their cooler, which they had netted well before crossing the Vermont border. "When we saw them," says Debra, "we said, 'We've never seen fish like that in this lake.'" A biologist assigned to the derby ended up proving it, because hatchery-raised fish contain implanted identifiers in their dorsal fins. They were also pretty well banged up from being contained in breeding tanks. "So we got U.S. Fish and Wildlife involved, because they had taken the fish over state lines and tried to submit them here. So they were hit with federal fines, as well."

Since 1995 the derby has been postponed five times until the end of February due to warm weather or rain. An ominous sign of global warming? "Well, it's irritating, to be sure," says Debra, "but it's out of my hands. I've been chairing the derby for five years. Now it's somebody else's turn."

★ ★ ★ ★ ★ ★ ★ ★ ★ ★ ★ ★ ★ ★ ★ ★ ★ ★ ★ ★ ★ ★ ★ ★ ★ ★ ★ ★ ★

Directions: The Harriman Reservoir is south of Wilmington, about 17 miles west of Brattleboro on Route 9. The Ice Derby is scheduled for the first weekend each February, weather permitting. For more information see the Deerfield Valley Sportsman's Club Web site at www.dvscvt.com/derby.html or call (802) 368-2908.

# 3

## *Southwest*

### At present, I am living in Vermont.
*—Robert Frost (from his poem "New Hampshire")*

**Early in this** *chapter you'll learn about two artistic mysteries and how they were solved. The first had to do with one of Norman Rockwell's most famous paintings. A copy of it masquerading as the real article fooled hundreds of thousands of museum visitors all over the world for more than forty years before a sharp-eyed viewer blew the whistle in 2002. The guilty replicator? One of Rockwell's dearest friends. Less than 20 miles south, on U.S. Route 7 a little over a decade earlier, Bennington Museum curators waited in vain for a shipment of Grandma Moses, paintings bequeathed by a recently deceased Pennsylvania florist and friend of the painter. Fourteen years later, the paintings arrived in two wooden crates addressed to the museum director. The only clue to their whereabouts? A cryptic note on purple mimeograph paper inside one of the crates.*

*Now who would have pegged Abraham Lincoln's eldest son as a zealous golfer and captain of industry? But that's what he became. And years after a number of summers in Vermont with his mother and brother (his dad wasn't able to take that much time off), Robert Todd Lincoln built a twenty-four-room house in Manchester for his wife and three children. But it was one of his granddaughters who showed a spirit reminiscent of Abe himself. Mary Lincoln Peggy Beckwith became known as the "Amelia Earhart of Vermont," routinely landing one of her three planes in a meadow near the house. Peggy was also an artist, photographer, guitarist, fencer, and cross-country skier. After three generations, you might say, the apple rolled back closer to the tree.*

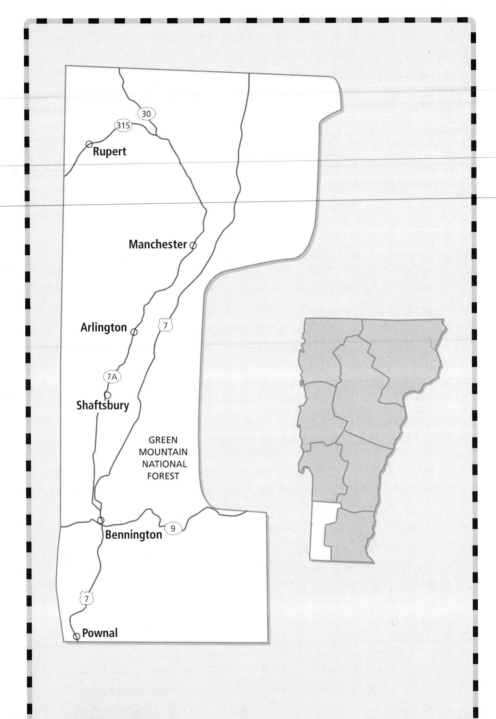

30

315

Rupert

Manchester

Arlington

7

7A

Shaftsbury

GREEN
MOUNTAIN
NATIONAL
FOREST

9

Bennington

7

Pownal

**SOUTHWEST**

★ ★ ★ ★ ★ ★ ★ ★ ★ ★ ★ ★ ★ ★ ★ ★ ★ ★ ★ ★ ★ ★ ★ ★ ★ ★ ★ ★ ★ ★ ★ ★ ★

## The Counterfeit Norman Rockwell—A Mystery

Arlington

Do any of you remember a Norman Rockwell painting —first seen on the cover of a 1954 issue of the *Saturday Evening Post*—depicting a boy waiting with his dad and his dog for the train taking him off to college for the first time? Even if so, you probably don't remember the title: It was *Breaking Home Ties.* The boy looks eagerly down the road. His rancher father, in denim and boots, sits resignedly beside him on the running board of their truck, holding his hat in his hands. They have said all there is to say. The family collie, head in its master's lap, is disconsolate.

In 1960 comic strip illustrator and artist Donald Trachte, a long-time friend and neighbor of Rockwell's in Arlington, bought *Breaking Home Ties* for $900 at a Southern Vermont Art Center exhibition of Rockwell's work. It remained one of his most prized possessions. Ten years later, when Trachte and his wife divorced, that painting was part of a collection of eight that was given to the children. The parents, though, were awarded temporary custody of the paintings in their respective homes. Trachte chose the Rockwell and hung it over his grand piano, when it wasn't on loan to museums all over the world, Cairo to Moscow. His ex-wife kept five of the other paintings in the collection. For the next forty years, dealers and collectors pursued Trachte and his four children about purchasing *Breaking Home Ties.*

When Trachte moved into an assisted-living home in 2002, the children transferred what they thought was the original to the Rockwell Museum, in Stockbridge, Massachusetts. Over the next three years, *Breaking Home Ties* was seen by hundreds of thousands of visitors to the museum.

Before it was exhibited, a preparatory cleaning revealed several small discrepancies from the original *Saturday Evening Post* cover tear sheet. Curators concluded that these were the effects of time and travel, however, rather than chicanery. Even so, in 2004, one expert called it "a third-rate replica."

★ ★ ★ ★ ★ ★ ★ ★ ★ ★ ★ ★ ★ ★ ★ ★ ★ ★ ★ ★ ★ ★ ★ ★ ★ ★ ★ ★ ★

Photo courtesy Don Trachte Jr.

**Moments before this photo was taken in 2006, brothers Don and Dave Trachte discovered the original Rockwell "Breaking Home Ties" painting in their dad's Arlington studio.**

"Wow," Dave Trachte remembers thinking at the time, "our one and only treasure and people think it's no good."

Then, in 2005, Don Trachte died, giving his four children total access to their dad's home and studio. Two months later, when all four children visited the studio just after their dad's memorial service, Don Jr. found two nearly identical versions of a George Hughes painting in the closet of the studio.

"So now we have two clues," says Don, "suspicions of a fake Rockwell and the duplicate George Hughes paintings. We suspected something, but we just weren't putting two-and-two together."

In January of 2006 Don got a call from a New York gallery again questioning the authenticity of the Rockwell painting. After driving to Stockbridge for another look at *Breaking Home Ties*, Don and Dave agreed that there were subtle differences in the boy's face between the painting and their photo of the original. A restoration expert found no indication that the painting had been altered, but Dave was still skeptical. In March, looking through the studio yet again, he noticed a gap in the paneling of a wall next to an inset bookcase. He was able to push it enough to reveal the edges of several small paintings and quickly called Don in Burlington. Don arrived the next day with "deconstruction tools," but Dave's smile told him they wouldn't be needed. He had discovered that the panel slid easily. Out appeared several original paintings, copies of which their mother had hung on her walls. They moved to a second panel. Slowly, the edge of a larger painting became visible. First they saw a dog's tail, then the truck, then the boy. The original *Breaking Home Ties!*

The Trachte children believe that their father's underlying motive was to protect the family inheritance. "I'm not surprised," said their mother when the boys told her the story.

The original, in mint condition after its forty-year rest behind a wall (as opposed to the Trachte version's wear and tear of several hundred thousand travel miles), was sold at Sotheby's in New York for $15.4 million. The Trachte version and other paintings in that collection are on display from time to time at various museums. Both Sotheby's and the Rockwell Museum remain mum about the location of the original *Breaking Home Ties*. No surprise, really.

## A Christmas Gift to Our Nation's Capitol

Bennington

In 1923 President Calvin Coolidge pushed a button lighting the first national Christmas tree—from Vermont, naturally. But that was in the days when there was only one national Christmas tree. Beginning in 1964, two trees went to Washington: one to the White House and

★ ★ ★ ★ ★ ★ ★ ★ ★ ★ ★ ★ ★ ★ ★ ★ ★ ★ ★ ★ ★ ★ ★ ★ ★ ★ ★ ★ ★ ★

one to the Capitol Building. In 1978 a blue spruce from Pennsylvania was planted near the White House as a permanent Christmas tree, but cut trees are still sent to the Capitol each December from one of a number of states with plentiful national forests.

The 2007 U.S. Capitol Christmas tree was another gift from the people of Vermont—their fifth Washington tree offering since 1923—and was cut in the Green Mountain National Forest (GMNF) near Somerset. The occasion also marked the GMNF's seventy-fifth anniversary. This graceful, 60-foot-tall balsam fir was selected twenty-seven years earlier by Bennington County forester Jim White and indulged like an only child from then on. Jim cut away nearby trees and brush to provide maximum opportunity for sunlight and growth. At appropriate intervals the tree was fed organic fertilizers and inoculated against arcane balsam diseases. White, now retired, has selected and coddled four such Washington-bound trees over the years.

The town of Somerset, with a population so low (five, according to the 2000 U.S. Census) that its affairs are handled by a state-appointed supervisor, had neither resources nor inclination to plan and execute the tree's journey. Woodford, the town next closest to the tree, is known both for being the highest and the oldest village in the state, but with a population of 363, it was similarly ill equipped to take on the task. It was up to nearby Bennington, a commercial hub in southwestern Vermont, to step up. And it did.

Eighteen months before the tree was cut, a committee of residents in and around Bennington was organized by the local chamber of commerce. Within weeks, led by cochairs Joann Erenhouse and Lindy Lynch, it conceived a twenty-two-vehicle caravan of antique trucks to carry the chosen tree—plus a spare—as well as ninety-five smaller trees and nearly 5,000 ornaments and pupil-produced greeting cards. The pair also attracted enough volunteers to spearhead all planning, funding, and publicity. Dave Zsido, a manager at Central Vermont Public Service, managed the harvesting of the tree and was tapped as trail boss for the trip down.

Photo courtesy of U.S. Senator Pat Leahy

Aloft at last! The 2007 Capitol Christmas tree is lit after twenty-seven years of pampering since its selection, and culminating in a delicately executed twenty-two-truck convoy to Washington, D.C.

The fund-raising and budgeting duties were directed by Don Keelan, a writer and CPA from nearby Arlington. Keelan brought the venture in at $125,000, no small feat, considering that two previous states, Virginia in 2004 and Michigan in 2001, had spent $647,000 and $1.1 million, respectively, on their trees.

The original intention was to distribute the ninety-five "companion trees" trees to government offices and officials in Washington. But during a fund-raising trip to the Vermont legislature in Montpelier early in 2006, Lieutenant Governor Brian Dubie suggested to the event cochairs that veterans in hospitals and homes along the way would be more worthy recipients than just government officials and offices.

★ ★ ★ ★ ★ ★ ★ ★ ★ ★ ★ ★ ★ ★ ★ ★ ★ ★ ★ ★ ★ ★ ★ ★ ★ ★ ★ ★ ★ ★

"Whenever I'm in D.C., I try to visit Walter Reed Army Medical Center," said Lieutenant Governor Dubie. "Conversations with our wounded soldiers and their families have had a profound effect on me. I also knew that visiting VA homes along the way would be appreciated by our veterans." As a result of Dubie's suggestion, the caravan visited five veterans' homes and three veterans' hospitals, including Walter Reed and the Armed Forces Retirement Home, in Washington.

Some of the publicity responsibilities for the Washington trip went to Don Keelan, in addition to his other duties. Fifteen times—at hospitals, veterans' homes, and community gatherings along the way—Keelan adopted his Smokey Bear persona to remind audiences of the importance of protecting America's forests. He also wrote newspaper columns chronicling the event's progress as plans began to jell.

The trip itself was masterfully choreographed, with no newsworthy glitches. A few branches from the Somerset tree were broken, but surgical repairs using the spare-parts tree were deftly performed by Capitol landscape specialists. Nobody was the wiser.

At the base of the tree, just before it was raised from horizontal to vertical, an anonymous joker had written a final instruction to the work crew—in permanent marker and 3-inch capital letters: THIS END DOWN.

Now people are looking forward to 2032, the Green Mountain National Forest's one hundredth anniversary. If Vermont is selected to provide a tree for that occasion—and there's every reason to believe it will be—this should be an even more unforgettable wingding.

Directions: While you can't see the tree itself, you can go to the Green Mountain National Forest, to the east of U.S. Route 7 between Vergennes and Rutland. For more information, visit www .fs.fed.us/r9/gmfl/.

# Moonlight in Vermont

The classic and haunting ballad "Moonlight in Vermont" was written by two non-Vermonters. John Blackburn, who wrote the lyrics, taught drama for two years at Bennington College. He teamed with composer Karl Suessdorf when both worked in Los Angeles during World War II.

Composer Johnny Mercer liked the melody and brought it to vocalist Margaret Whiting in 1945. It created little splash, but when Whiting rerecorded the song ten years later, it made the top ten. It was subsequently recorded by such artists as Frank Sinatra, Ella Fitzgerald, Billie Holliday, Ray Charles, and Willie Nelson. In 1985 Vermont's legislature decreed a "Moonlight in Vermont Day," and Whiting made her first trip to the state to sing the song before a joint session of the legislature.

In the late 1990s this same legislature rejected "Moonlight in Vermont" as the official state song, partly, it was said, because it was too difficult for the average person to sing.

## The Grandma Moses Museum Heist

Bennington

Here's how it went down: Anna Mary Robertson Moses began to paint seriously at age seventy-six, and in 1939 a New York art collector saw samples of her work displayed in a Hoosick Falls, New York, drugstore, 5 miles from her home in Eagle Bridge. This led to a one-woman show in 1940 and established Grandma Moses, as she was called, as a fixture in the history of American art.

★ ★ ★ ★ ★ ★ ★ ★ ★ ★ ★ ★ ★ ★ ★ ★ ★ ★ ★ ★ ★ ★ ★ ★ ★ ★

Margaret Carr and Ruth Garner, sisters who ran a florist shop in Rose Valley, Pennsylvania, just outside Philadelphia, met Grandma Moses in 1952. They loved her work. Over the next few years, they paid her several visits, usually buying one or more paintings, either by the artist herself or by her son, Forrest King Moses. Eventually they became friends, talking by phone twice a year, sending gifts, and occasionally visiting Grandma Moses at her home in Eagle Bridge, where she occasionally gave them a painting they admired.

On December 13, 1961, Grandma Moses died at the age of 101. She left her sister-friends a sofa and other memorabilia to commemorate their friendship. When Margaret Carr died in 1984, she bequeathed seven of the artist's paintings to the Bennington Museum, plus the sofa, letters, clippings, and other gifts they had received over the years.

In 1972, the New York schoolhouse attended by Grandma Moses was moved to the Bennington Museum. It explores her work.

Mrs. Carr had made meticulous arrangements to ship the paintings and other materials to the museum. So far as the museum knew, the shipment was on its way, but it never arrived. At different times investigators from the Pennsylvania State Police, the FBI, and the Galerie St. Etienne in New York City all went to Mrs. Carr's home in Rose Valley and found the two Forrest Moses paintings, the sofa, and memorabilia. The seven Grandma Moses paintings had disappeared. All leads in the case dead-ended right there, and that's how the matter stood for the next fourteen years.

Curator Jamie Franklin filled in the story from there. "On February 9, 1998, the seven paintings arrived at the Bennington Museum in two wooden crates addressed to Director Steve Miller from a commercial shipping company in Quakerstown, Pennsylvania," said Franklin. "A cryptic note on purple mimeograph paper was signed 'Ring Sar,' and attempts to trace the source of both the shipment and the shippers were unsuccessful."

All of the information the shippers provided the shipping company turned out to be false. Best guess is that the heist was perpetrated by a person or persons who had known Margaret Carr, as well as about the will, including the paintings' final destination. Because the paintings were kept in excellent condition and no paper trail exists that attempts were made to sell them over the fourteen years, a further guess is that the thieves were not interested in making a profit, but simply enjoyed the artist's work. A clean getaway!

The Bennington Museum holds the largest collection of art by Grandma Moses. Great-grandson Will Moses is continuing the family folk art tradition at the Mt. Nebo Gallery, in Eagle Bridge, New York.

Directions: The Bennington Museum is in downtown Bennington at 75 Main Street (Route 9). The museum is open 10:00 a.m. to 5:00 p.m., with days of the week varying by season. See www.bennington museum.org for the best information or call (802) 447-1571.

# When You Don't Want to Settle for a Rolls-Royce

Between 1920 and 1924 only eighteen Martin-Wasps were produced. Now this was the motor car to consider if a Pierce-Arrow or a Rolls-Royce wasn't exclusive enough for you. Karl H. Martin, a successful automobile coachwork designer for a number of New York companies, wanted to design and market an auto of his own. He went back to his hometown of Bennington, leased part of a foundry, and, with the help of a couple of financial backers, founded the Martin-Wasp Corporation.

Martin put twenty-eight people on his payroll, most of whom built the chassis of the Wasp by hand. All of his early models featured twin spare tires and a Saint Christopher's medal embedded in the dashboard. Martin created several body styles but priced them all at $10,000, which comes to just under $113,000 in today's dollars. At the New York Auto Show in 1920, screen star Douglas Fairbanks Jr. (who was first to leave footprints in wet cement outside Hollywood's Grauman's Chinese Theatre) bought a Wasp from Martin. But in 1924 one of Martin's principal backers died, and he closed down production.

Today the sole remaining Martin-Wasp is on display at the Bennington Museum. It was totally restored in the 1960s and still looks pretty spiffy with its dark green body and maroon wheels. I wasn't able to get an answer as to whether it could still maintain its original top speed of 15 miles per hour.

### The One, the Only Covered Bridge Museum

Bennington

Just reading from the promotion here: "Discover the exciting history, culture, nature, science, and art of covered bridges in the first and only museum dedicated to the preservation of these wonderful structures."

*First*, I'm inclined to give them, but *only*? That might be a stretch. But then I think: A covered bridge that itself is a covered bridge museum, even if it is a reproduction . . . maybe we do have us an "only."

It is a magical experience to go across a covered bridge for the first time, especially if you take a few minutes to examine the level of craftsmanship that went into its construction. The Vermont Covered

The Covered Bridge Museum is an exact replica of a town lattice bridge. It is connected—psychically and physically—to the Bennington Center for the Natural and Cultural Arts.

★ ★ ★ ★ ★ ★ ★ ★ ★ ★ ★ ★ ★ ★ ★ ★ ★ ★ ★ ★ ★ ★ ★ ★ ★ ★ ★ ★ ★ ★ ★ ★ ★ ★ ★

Bridge Museum gives you an opportunity for this and provides 3-D models, dioramas, and a working covered bridge railroad layout to show in realistic detail what these bridges could do and how they did it. You can even sit at one of two computer workstations to build and test your own covered bridge design.

The original purpose of the covered bridge was not to keep travelers from nasty weather. Its enclosing roof protected the timbers from weathering, which prolonged the life of the bridge. Nevertheless, this natural shelter was also used as a gathering place or picnic location. Covered bridges also were considered to be great boxing rings. It is said that Norwich University moved from Norwich to Northfield, Vermont, in an attempt to stop boxing matches on the Ledyard Bridge between its students and those of Dartmouth College.

Here's the skinny on the cost of crossing a Vermont river in the 1800s, when a covered bridge was between you and the other side ("A brief darkness leading from the light to light," as Henry Wadsworth Longfellow put it a bit more lyrically):

### 1800s COVERED BRIDGE BILL OF FARE

| | |
|---|---|
| A man on foot | 1 cent |
| A man on horseback | 4 cents |
| A one-horse carriage | 10 cents |
| A carriage drawn by more than one horse | 20 cents |
| Cattle | 1 cent (driver free) |
| Sheep or swine | ½ cent (driver free) |

Directions: The Vermont Covered Bridge Museum is located at 44 Gypsy Lane at Route 9 in Bennington and is part of the Bennington Center for the Arts. The museum is open 10:00 a.m.–5:00 p.m., Tuesday–Sunday. Check out www.benningtoncenterforthearts.org/vtCBM/ for a wide variety of information, or call (802) 442-7158.

## Would Abe Lincoln Have Slept Here?

Manchester

There's no way to break this other than just come right out with it: Abraham Lincoln's oldest son was a passionate golfer and a corporate titan. It seems the apple fell a good distance from the tree.

Most think this all started when Lincoln enrolled Robert at Harvard in 1861, the same year he took office as president. After his father's death Robert Todd Lincoln parlayed an inheritance of $110,000 or so (about $1.75 million in today's dollars), his name, and a law degree into a position as special counsel for the Pullman Corporation. In 1901, after George Pullman died, Lincoln was named president of the company. In less than a decade, he took Pullman from a $300,000 company to a $10 million company. (That's the "coporate titan" part.)

Today the home and grounds of Robert Lincoln serve as hub for activities such as children's camps, craft festivals, art shows, fairs, and concerts.

Robert Lincoln also served as secretary of war under presidents James Garfield and Chester A. Arthur, and as ambassador to the United Kingdom under President Benjamin Harrison. Retiring in 1922, he made his last public appearance in Washington, D.C., in that same year for the dedication ceremony for his father's memorial.

Robert's love for the Manchester area began back in 1863, while his dad was president. That summer, as well as the following year, his mother, his brother, Tad, and he stayed at the Equinox Hotel, which still displays a copy of the guestbook page on which Mary Todd Lincoln registered. Mrs. Lincoln booked the entire family for the summer of 1865, a trip that the president did not live to take. In 1905, after spending more and more time in Manchester during the summers, Robert, his wife, and their three children moved into a twenty-four-room mansion they had built on 500 acres of land in the Battenkill Valley, smack-dab between Vermont's Green Mountains and the Taconic Range in New York. Robert's wife, Mary Harlan, named the house Hildene, an amalgam of two Old English words that together mean "hill and valley." The expansive front yard made a great driving range, where Robert was able to polish his long game between matches at the local country club. (That's the "passionate golfer" part.)

Of their three children Abraham "Jack" Lincoln II died at sixteen of blood poisoning. Because the other two children were girls, this ended the family name, but not the line of descendants. Daughter Jessie Harlan Lincoln married three times and produced a son and a daughter. The daughter, Mary Lincoln "Peggy" Beckwith, called Hildene home her whole life. The following paragraphs were written from notes taken during a conversation with Gary Sloan, a leading Hildene interpreter.

Peggy remained single and childless, perhaps leery of the experiences of both her mother and her brother, who married six times between them. But she did manage to cram a lot of living into her time at Hildene. She was a serious farmer and raised Black Angus cattle and dairy herds on the property. At times she kept several dogs and cats and adopted a couple of baby raccoons.

But she also had a passion as strong as her grandfather Robert's was for the game of golf. And Peggy loved mechanized vehicles. She

★ ★ ★ ★ ★ ★ ★ ★ ★ ★ ★ ★ ★ ★ ★ ★ ★ ★ ★ ★ ★ ★ ★ ★ ★

is said to have gone through several cars a year—sometimes buying back those she sold and then missed so much she realized she couldn't part with them.

Her reputation was even more prominent, however, as the "Amelia Earhart of Vermont." Between 1928 and 1933 Peggy owned as many as three single-engine two-place planes, taking off and landing from an airfield on the meadows by the farm. Her grandmother, Robert Todd's widow, was violently opposed to her granddaughter flying around in "one of those machines." Peggy convinced her grandmother to agree to a test: Peggy would land her plane in the front yard and prove that this was a safe and proper hobby, and that she (Peggy) was not in grave danger. But apparently Peggy failed the test. She landed safely but was unable to make a case good enough to change her grandmother's mind. That was the last of the flying in and about Hildene.

But Peggy remained a well-known figure about town and looked like anything but a millionaire, her in-town outfit usually consisting of overalls and boots. Children loved her, though, and sons and daughters of staff members could be found weekends watching *Howdy Doody* or the *Beverly Hillbillies* around her television set. When the kids got thirsty, there was a Coke machine nearby.

Mary Lincoln Peggy Beckwith was also an artist and an accomplished photographer. She fenced, she loved cross-country skiing, she played guitar, and she composed for the piano. You have to believe she would have been a source of delight to her great-granddad.

Directions: On U.S. Route 7, take exit 3 (Route 313) toward Arlington. Turn right on Vermont Route 7A. Travel north for about 8 miles, and turn right onto Hildene Road. Hildene is open daily 9:30 a.m. to 4:30 p.m. For more information visit www.hildene.org or call the Friends of Hildene at (802) 362-1788.

★ ★ ★ ★ ★ ★ ★ ★ ★ ★ ★ ★ ★ ★ ★ ★ ★ ★ ★ ★ ★ ★ ★ ★ ★ ★ ★ ★ ★ ★ ★ ★

## A Black Veterans' Museum in the Nation's Whitest State
Pownal

A scant one-half of one percent of Vermont's population consists of African Americans. Yet the state is still the location of the nation's only museum devoted to the heroism and military exploits of black soldiers, sailors, and marines.

Founder Bruce Bird is neither black nor a veteran; he is someone who saw a major part of American history hardly being addressed. He explains, "I've been studying military history for fifty-five years, and thinking about a museum since the 1980s. Then about five years ago, it occurred to me that 1.2 million African Americans served in the military during World War II, and that nobody was talking about it, other than through an occasional book. So if I'm going to do a museum, why not that, because no one else is doing it."

But why Vermont? "Because I was born here."

You wouldn't consider any other state? "There are other places that might be better for the business, but I don't have the money." But even if someone wanted to buy the museum to take it elsewhere, Bruce says they'd have to take him along with it.

As to the exhibits:

"The Tuskegee Airmen (332nd Fighter Group) are really the royalty of the black servicemen in World War II," says Bruce, so it is no wonder an exhibit dedicated to them makes up one of the highlights of the museum. From 1942 through 1946, nearly 1,000 pilots received commissions and pilot wings at Tuskegee Army Airfield. Many thousands more bombardiers, navigators, and gunnery crews were trained at other air bases across the country. Because of the rampant racism and bigotry of the time, these men fought two wars—one against a military enemy overseas, and the other against bigotry both at home and abroad. Even so, they compiled an outstanding record. In more than 200 missions over Germany, not a single bomber was lost to enemy fighters.

"But there were an awful lot of other people doing other things who got absolutely no recognition anywhere, and they suffered as much and died just as dead as anybody else," says Bruce. To commemorate these men and women, and hundreds of thousands more, Bird has assembled their photos, artifacts, and dramatic narratives in what used to be Pownal's Oak Hill School, which dates back to the nineteenth century. He is also on call from schools and community groups to speak about the museum and this period in our history.

Photo courtesy Museum of Black WW II History

**Founder and curator Bruce Bird has filled a gap in our nation's history by highlighting the exploits of more than one million Black World War II veterans who served with distinction.**

Directions: The museum is on Oak Hill School Road, which is off of Vermont Route 7 8.5 miles south of Bennington. Drive west on the road 1/10 mile and the museum will be on your right at 179 Oak Hill School Road. The museum is open Monday–Thursday, 10:00 a.m. –5:00 p.m. year-round. Admission is charged. For more information visit www.blackww2museum.org, or call (802) 823-5519.

## "I Had a Lover's Quarrel with the World"

Shaftsbury

Robert Frost's headstone inscription succinctly summarizes the great disparity between his professional successes and personal tragedies over a lifetime of nearly eighty-nine years. His first moneymaking poem was published when he was twenty, he was the first writer to be awarded four Pulitzer Prizes, he lectured internationally, and in 1961 the Vermont legislature named him the poet laureate of Vermont.

On the other hand, Frost's father died when the poet was eleven (leaving the family with $8 after expenses were paid), Frost's first son died at age four (and his mother six months later), his fourth

Robert Frost moved from New Hampshire to Vermont in 1920. One reason: On the eighty acres of farmland, he could grow "a thousand apple trees of some unforbidden variety."

daughter died after three days, his sister was committed to an insane asylum and later died there, his second daughter died a day after her first daughter was born, and his second son committed suicide.

Although Frost is described as a Vermont poet, he was born in San Francisco, lived in Massachusetts until age twelve, finished high school in New Hampshire (at the head of his class, when he was fifteen), lived in New Hampshire and Massachusetts after he was married, and moved to London with his wife and two remaining children for two years to write full-time; but then he moved back to Massachusetts again and then Michigan and finally, when he was fifty-five, to Shaftsbury, Vermont.

The Robert Frost Stone House Museum in Shaftsbury contains galleries in the house where Frost both lived and wrote some of his best poetry. One of his most famous poems, "Stopping by Woods on a Snowy Evening," was composed on a sweltering June morning at his dining room table. Other Stone House exhibits include the J. J. Lankes Gallery, featuring woodcuts of Frost's favorite illustrator, and the bookshop offering books, recordings, and posters. Frost's grave is located nearby in Old Bennington.

Directions: From Main Street in Bennington, go north on U.S. Route 7 to exit 2, Shaftsbury. At end of ramp, turn right onto Vermont Route 7A and go north. Go 3/4 mile past Hiland Hall School. The museum is on the left side, at 121 Historic Route 7A. The Stone House Museum is open from May to November, 10:00 a.m.–5:00 p.m., Tuesday–Sunday. For more information visit www.frostfriends .org or call (802) 447-6200.

# Escaping Vermont Winters without Moving a Muscle

Volume IV of the *Bulletin of the New York Public Library* lists ten separate disputes between New York and Vermont from 1780 until 1899 to fix the precise location of Vermont's western boundary. For example, in 1814 that line was moved westward some 50 feet from the border established two years earlier. According to Warren S. Patrick, one Rupert farmer affected by this particular surveyor's decision realized that his house and land were now entirely in the state of New York. "Thank God," he said to his wife. "I don't think I could stand another Vermont winter."

# 4

## *East Central*

**Let's start with** *Phineas Gage, a hardworking railroad foreman. One day in 1846, while setting dynamite charges to blast rock from the route of a track-construction project near Cavendish, Gage was distracted by a fellow worker and rammed his thirteen-pound tamping rod directly onto the dynamite stick—before the hole had been filled with a protective sand cover. The resulting blast knocked the rod back up through Gage's cheekbone and out the top of his skull. And that's when his new life began. Well into the next century, on the other side of Cavendish, recently exiled Soviet writer Aleksandr Solzhenitsyn was starting a new life in Vermont with his wife and three boys, with quite mixed results, as you'll see.*

*For a change of pace, find out how the Springfield Simpsons chose Vermont as their new home. Or . . . moving right along here, how a half dozen college kids helped Vermont win a fifteen-year war against the outdoor-advertising industry to become the first state in the union to eliminate billboard blight. All this plus scintillating tours through Vermont's oldest and only employee-owned flour company, an interactive science museum, a rescue haven for wounded birds of prey, and the small Vermont hill town of Plymouth Notch, virtually unchanged from the days that President Coolidge ran his summer White House there, in the dance hall above his father's general store.*

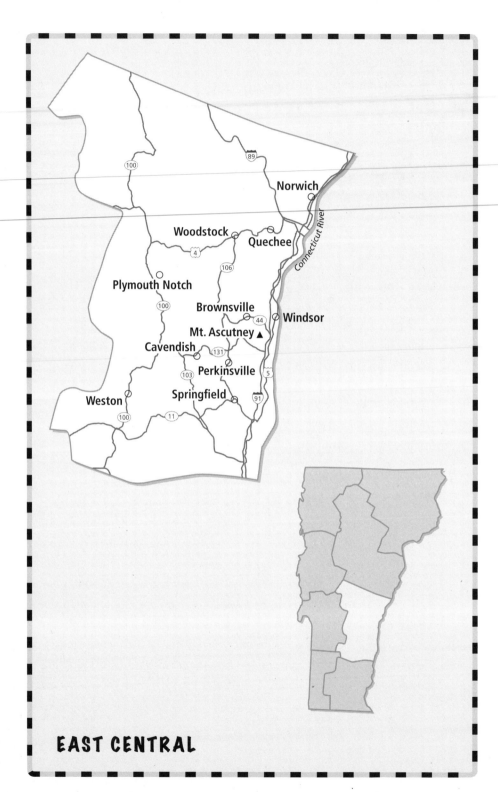

Norwich

Woodstock

Quechee

Connecticut River

Plymouth Notch

Brownsville

Windsor

Mt. Ascutney ▲

Cavendish

Perkinsville

Weston

Springfield

**EAST CENTRAL**

## Aleksandr Solzhenitsyn—Reluctant Vermont Resident

Cavendish

He was an artillery captain and fought the Nazis in World War II. But in 1945, after writing a letter criticizing Joseph Stalin, Aleksandr Solzhenitsyn was sentenced to eight years in prison and three more in enforced exile. In 1956 he settled in central Russia, where he taught mathematics and began to write.

In 1962 Solzhenitsyn submitted a short novel describing life in the forced labor camps of the Stalin era. *One Day in the Life of Ivan Denisovich* was an immediate sensation and inspired other writers to tell their own stories of imprisonment under Stalin's rule.

For the next twelve years Solzhenitsyn continued to write critically of the Stalin regime, to acclaim abroad and criticism at home. In 1970 he was awarded the Nobel Prize for Literature but dared not go to Stockholm to receive it for fear of being barred from returning to the Soviet Union. For his scorching indictment of prisons and labor camps (*The Gulag Archipelago*) in 1974, Solzhenitsyn was arrested for treason and exiled the following day.

But why choose Cavendish? Initially, Solzhenitsyn's first choice was Zurich, Switzerland. But people who found out where he lived continually asked him for favors, when all he wanted was peace and time to write. His second choice was the United States, and a lawyer suggested Cavendish, in the wooded and sparsely populated Green Mountain region of Vermont, not too different an atmosphere from his beloved Russia. He moved there in 1976.

"There is one more reason I came to live here," Solzhenitsyn told French journalist Bernard Pivot, one of the few to interview the writer while he lived in the United States. "It is the extraordinary wealth of American universities regarding Russian manuscripts, books, and documents pertaining to the 1917 revolution."

For the next eighteen years, Aleksandr Solzhenitsyn and his family lived in Cavendish. His wife, Natalia, served as his archivist, typist, and advisor and helped raise their three boys. The writer finished volumes

★ ★ ★ ★ ★ ★ ★ ★ ★ ★ ★ ★ ★ ★ ★ ★ ★ ★ ★ ★ ★ ★ ★ ★ ★ ★ ★

two and three of *The Gulag Archipelago*, two other books of nonfiction, and four volumes of *The Red Wheel*, a history of the Russian revolution of 1917.

Solzhenitsyn and his wife then returned to Russia in 1994, where the author died in 2008. The boys, however, stayed to finish their education and became U.S. citizens. They still own the Vermont family home on Brook Road, in Cavendish. Ignat, a world-renowned pianist, is music director for the Chamber Orchestra of Philadelphia. He returned to his home state in 2007 to play an all-Brahms program in Brattleboro. His older brother Yermolay, who married a Russian girl, lives in Moscow and works at a U.S. firm. Younger brother Stephan is an environmental consultant in New York. "The interest in the Solzhenitzyns doesn't seem to die down," says Rich Svec, town manager of Cavendish. "Just a few months ago, a Russian film crew was here preparing a documentary examining their lives in the U.S."

Directions: To reach Cavendish, take exit 8 on I-91. Go west on Route 131 for 13 miles.

### Phineas Gage—He Needed This Job like a Hole in the Head
Cavendish

Bolted to a rock on Pleasant Street is a plaque commemorating "The Gage Accident." It was placed there in 1998, 150 years after a story that goes like this:

On September 13, 1848, Phineas P. Gage, a twenty-five-year-old Rutland & Burlington Railroad construction foreman, was setting dynamite charges to remove rock ledges impeding the railroad's expansion across Vermont. He first drilled a narrow hole in the rock and filled it halfway with blasting powder. Next came a fuse, and finally the powder was covered with protective sand and tamped down. Gage customarily signaled one of his men to pour in the sand before he tamped it down, with a rod designed for him by a local blacksmith. On this afternoon, however, he gestured for his partner to put in the sand and then was distracted by another worker. When

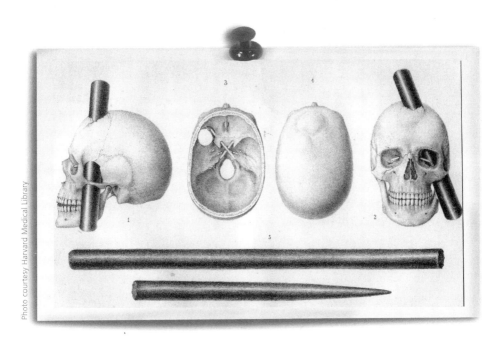

Imagine what poor Phineas thought when these x-rays came in. Oh, right. X-rays hadn't been invented yet. (These pictures are from a "prepared cranium.")

he looked back and rammed his thirteen-pound tamping rod into the hole, he failed to see that his partner had not yet added the sand. His rod struck rock, created a spark, and whammo!

A tremendous blast propelled the 3-foot, 7-inch rod through Gage's left cheekbone, exiting the top of his skull at high speed, and landing, covered with blood and brains, more than 100 feet behind him. When his fellow workers reached the stunned Gage, they were amazed to see that he was not only alive but conscious. They carried him to an ox-drawn cart, which took him the three-quarters of a mile back to Cavendish. He was erect and got up the steps to the Adams Hotel with just a little assistance. According to neurobiologist Antonio Damasio, in his book *Descartes' Error*, when the doctor arrived at Adams Hotel, Gage was seated on the front porch and greeted him by saying, "Doctor, here is business enough for you."

★ ★ ★ ★ ★ ★ ★ ★ ★ ★ ★ ★ ★ ★ ★ ★ ★ ★ ★ ★ ★ ★ ★ ★ ★ ★ ★ ★

He was under the doctor's care for ten weeks and then discharged to his home in Lebanon, New Hampshire. Within two months he had completely recovered: He could walk, speak, and was pain free.

But it was soon clear that the Phineas Gage who went back to work was a completely different man. The hardworking, responsible, and popular Phineas was now, as his doctor wrote, ". . . fitful, irreverent, indulging in the grossest profanity . . . pertinaciously obstinate, yet capricious and vacillating. . . .[H]is mind was radically changed, so decidedly that his friends and acquaintances said he was 'no longer Gage.'"

Phineas was fired from his job in 1850 and spent about a year as a sideshow attraction at P. T. Barnum's New York museum, displaying his scars—and the tamping iron that caused them—to anyone willing to pay for the privilege. His health began to fail in 1859, and he moved to San Francisco to live with his mother. In 1860 he began to have epileptic seizures and died a few months later at the age of forty-two, buried with the rod that damaged him.

In 1990 an autopsy on Gage's exhumed body by Drs. Antonio and Hanna Damasio confirmed that the ruinous damage to the frontal lobes by the rod is what caused Gage's antisocial behavior, and that the seizures leading to his death were accident-related as well. Both his skull and the rod are part of a permanent exhibition at Harvard Medical School's Warren Anatomical Museum in Boston, Massachusetts.

In 1998, at the 150th commemoration of the tragic explosion, Phineas's rod was brought by armed guard from Harvard to Cavendish for the ceremony.

Directions: To reach Cavendish, take exit 8 on I-91. Go west on Route 131 for 13 miles. The memorial plaque is in an empty lot at the corner of Route 131 and Pleasant Street. For more information and pictures, go to www.roadsideamerica.com/story/10858.

## America's Oldest Flour Company Is Not Showing Its Age

Norwich

As soon as you hit the front door, you know that the folks at King Arthur Flour have things under control—in a nice way. On one wall is a video of a master baker giving instruction in the proper kneading of what will soon be a scrumptious loaf of bread. And he's right. Even with the sound off, I am aware that my technique needs help. I definitely could be more relaxed and allow the dough to stretch on its own, rather than pummeling it into submission as is my practice. I promise myself to be gentler with the limpa (Swedish rye bread) I

Among the gazillion other specialties and recipes, some going back more than 200 years, pizza definitely is on King Arthur Flour's radar—including recipes. Monitor its URL to see.

bake next Christmas season. Ten feet from the TV monitor and under a glass-covered dome are free olive bread samples. Mmmm.

History first. The company was born in 1790 as the Sands, Taylor, and Wood Company, selling flour by the barrel off Long Wharf in Boston. It changed its name to King Arthur Flour after the owners saw a performance of King Arthur and the Knights of the Round Table. The extension of that metaphor within King Arthur Flour has since reached dizzying proportions, which need not concern us here.

All King Arthur flours have been free of bleach or chemicals of any kind for more than 200 years, which alone would qualify this company as a curiosity. Three of its eight flours are 100 percent organic. The company also sells a line of baking equipment, ingredients, mixes, and fresh-baked goods both in the store and through its *Baker's Catalogue*. (Shipped baked goods are sent express.)

The press kit, courtesy of media coordinator Allison Furbish, tells us that the bakery produces up to 400 loaves of bread on a weekday, 600 on a weekend day, and that a team of eight bakers crank out the product in shifts of two. They start so early in the morning (3:00) that their lunch hour (actually only a half hour) is at 9:00. The pastry makers begin at 4:00 a.m., and each day bake dozens of different pastries for the Baker's Store and local inns and restaurants. (The daily bread-baking schedule customarily lists an average of six varieties.) On the day we visited, bread bakers Martin Philip and Becca Lambert were just finishing up batches of baguettes and Sonnenblumenbrot (or sunflower-seed bread). Martin bagged one of those five-syllable loaves just for me. Tasty!

In addition to straight baking, the company maintains a hotline staffed by eight seasoned bakers who answer 61,000 calls and e-mails a year from bakers with problems. Rebecca Faill, a cooking-school graduate and former caterer, has heard it all, from a woman trying to duplicate her neighbor's award-winning pie to a monk fine-tuning a bread recipe for his monastery.

Directions: King Arthur's Flour is a gray building with red trim located on U.S. Route 5, 1/2 mile south of I-91 exit 13, on the left just past the car dealership. The Baker's Store is located at 135 Route 5 South, Norwich, Vermont. Store hours are Monday–Saturday, 8:30 a.m.– 6:00 p.m. and Sunday, 8:30 a.m.– 4:00 p.m. Read more about King Arthur Flour and its many services on www.kingarthurflour.com or call (802) 649-3361.

### Science a Kid Can Groove On
Norwich

Waiting at the front desk for curatorial assistant Heidi Fassnacht to tell me about the Montshire Museum of Science, I saw a six-year-old dart from behind an exhibit 20 feet away to retrieve a yellow ping-pong ball from the carpeted floor. Then another. And another. I walked closer to see what the breakdown might be. Then I saw the boy's father, on his knees, putting those balls into a "Tube Tunnel" that demonstrated one of a number of air-pressure-related physics principles. It was then that I first appreciated the museum's laid-back, interactive genius.

More than sixty hands-on exhibits relating to the natural sciences, astronomy, ecology, and technology can be found both inside and out

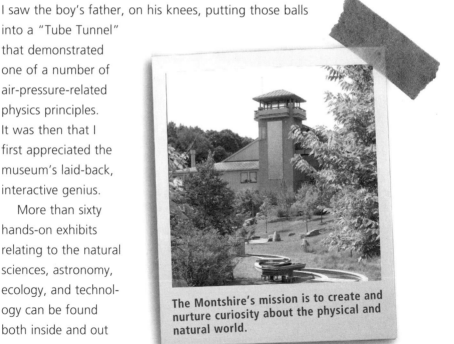

The Montshire's mission is to create and nurture curiosity about the physical and natural world.

on the museum's 110-acre site. In addition to the permanent exhibits, revolving exhibits are maintained for several months at a time to highlight current developments in science or provide a local venue for exhibits traveling among several major cities. "Toys: The Inside Story," for example, revealed how pulleys, circuits, gears, cams, and other mechanisms make familiar toys, such as an Etch-a-Sketch or a jack-in-the-box, work.

A network of nature trails includes a number of additional exhibits, the Human Sundial, and the Planet Walk, which requires a 1.6-mile hike to reach Pluto.

The Montshire is designed to appeal to all ages, like an animated movie produced to attract both adults and children. Most indoor exhibit spaces and all restrooms are wheelchair accessible, as are the walking trails.

Directions: The Montshire is located off I-91, exit 13, 5 miles north of White River Junction, directly across the Connecticut River from Dartmouth College in New Hampshire, at 1 Monstshire Road. The museum is open daily, 10:00 a.m. to 5:00 p.m. For more information go to www.montshire.org, or call (802) 649-2200.

### The President Coolidge Summer Home—Just above His Store
Plymouth Notch

Back in President Coolidge's day there were no grand presidential libraries. His papers, and those of his predecessors, are in the Library of Congress. But let's say there were—grand presidential libraries, that is. Chances are that rather than raise millions of dollars for a monument to himself, our thirtieth president more likely would have refurbished the Wilder Barn on his property and replaced the agricultural equipment exhibition that now occupies it with appropriate records of his years in the White House.

Bill Jenney, regional historic site administrator at the birthplace and boyhood home of Calvin Coolidge, recounts the night that the presidential guard was changed: "In August of 1923, when Vice

The Coolidge birthplace bedroom looks exactly as it did on July 4, 1872, when Calvin Coolidge was born. The chamber pot rests at lower right.

President Coolidge happened to be up here visiting his family, word came that President Warren Harding had died. [Coolidge] had to be sworn in immediately, and the only available official was his father, who was also the local notary public. Actually, there was a second ceremony with a federal judge back in Washington, because there was some debate as to whether a state official could swear in a federal officer. That Coolidge was sworn in by his father in the family homestead, in the middle of the night, by the light of a kerosene lamp, played quite well in the presidential campaign for the 1924 election, when he ran in his own right, and which he won with the highest plurality then known."

★ ★ ★ ★ ★ ★ ★ ★ ★ ★ ★ ★ ★ ★ ★ ★ ★ ★ ★ ★ ★ ★ ★ ★ ★ ★ ★ ★ ★

John Calvin Coolidge Jr. was born on July 4, 1872, within yards of the room in which his father swore him in as president. He graduated from Amherst College with honors and entered law and politics in Northampton, Massachusetts. Some think that because Coolidge was an accidental president, he had little taste for the top office. But slowly and methodically, he went up the Republican political ladder, from councilman in Northampton to governor of Massachusetts. His forceful intervention in the Boston police strike of 1919 propelled him to national attention, and President Warren G. Harding named him as his running mate in the 1920 election. Twenty-nine months later, Harding died of a heart attack at fifty-seven.

The small Vermont hill town of Plymouth Notch is virtually unchanged from the days during which President Coolidge ran his summer White House here in the dance hall above his father's general store. His entire staff consisted of a secretary and a stenographer. The last summer before his reelection, however, this threesome was augmented by a Secret Service detail of eighteen, because of death threats Coolidge had received. That summer he also was recovering from the death of his son, also Calvin Jr., whose infected blister from playing tennis at the White House courts with his brother John led to blood poisoning. Coolidge declined to run for a second term on his own, believing that his one year in office after Harding's death should count as a full term.

The homes of Coolidge's family and neighbors on the site are carefully preserved, as are the village church, general store, and cheese factory—still making cheese using the original 1890 recipe. Also on-site are a visitors' center, two museum stores, two walking trails, a restaurant, and a picnic area. To visit the steep, hillside cemetery where Calvin Coolidge rests with seven generations of his family, turn right out of the visitors' parking area onto Route 100A, and turn left onto Lynds Hill Road, about 100 yards south.

Directions: The President Calvin Coolidge State Historic Site is located 6 miles south of U.S. Route 4 on State Route 100A. The site is open from the last weekend in May until mid-October, daily 9:30 a.m. to 5:00 p.m. For more specific information and to see a list of events, go to www.historicvermont.org/coolidge or call (802) 672-3773.

## Quechee Gorge, Vermont's "Little Grand Canyon"
Quechee

As a matter of scale, *minuscule* is probably more accurate a word than *little*, if Quechee Gorge and the Grand Canyon are being used in the same sentence. As a part of 600-acre Quechee Gorge State Park, it is still the most spectacular river gorge in Vermont. Just east of Quechee Village, the Ottauquechee River turns south and plunges into the narrow, rocky cleft of Quechee Gorge—165 feet deep and more than a mile long.

At right can be seen the result of erosion so massive it moved the Outtauquechee River waterfall far enough north to create Quechee Gorge.

Quechee Gorge is what remains of a waterfall that carved its way north over thousands of years, eroding tough metamorphic rock until the formidable barrier was cut clean through.

Enter the path along the gorge just north of the east side of the U.S. Route 4 bridge. To the right is a picnic area, and a quarter mile farther is the old Dewey Wool Mill, no longer in operation, and the waterfall that made it work. Walking back under the bridge will take

you to the gorge outlook, but be careful. This walk is more strenuous than the one to Dewey Wool Mill.

About 1,500 feet before the bridge (on the left going toward Woodstock) is Quechee Gorge State Park Campground.

Directions: Quechee Gorge can be reached by taking exit 1 on Interstate 89 toward Woodstock, and then going 7 miles southeast on U.S. Route 4. Admission is free. An annual highlight is the Quechee Gorge Hot Air Balloon Festival on Father's Day weekend. Thousands attend, so if you're interested, make reservations early. For more information visit the park's Web site at www.vtstateparks.com/htm/quechee.cfm.

## Vermont Home for Wounded Birds of Prey
Quechee

There's a lot more to the Vermont Institute of Natural Science (VINS) than its rescue program for raptors and songbirds, but that seems its best-known activity. Each year more than 400 hawks and hummingbirds, geese and grackles, waxwings and warblers are welcomed to the nature center and rehabilitated. Some are highway hit-and-run victims; others have collided with a window; still others arrive orphaned, with no visible means of support. A number of other rehabilitation specialists with ties to VINS throughout the state and in New Hampshire are on call for the rescue and rehab of hundreds more, as well as a like number of mammals.

"We ask questions to find out what the injury might be, and whether the bird actually needs assistance or not," says Stephanie Hanwell, lead wildlife keeper and one of the specialists on call. "In the summer, for example, we get lots of baby-bird calls. When they're fledglings, they're just out hopping on their own, even though their parents are still taking care of them. But because they're not able to fly more than a foot or two, sometimes people think they're injured." A lot of deductive questioning determines the next step: whether to refer the caller to a local rehabilitator or, if the caller is reporting an injured mammal (the Quechee center takes in only birds), to refer them to the appropriate rehabber, or to one of the ten or so veterinarians throughout the state who work with VINS.

About 50 percent of the birds treated can be released in the wild again. Some die, of course, and the rest—primarily raptors—are either put up for adoption or kept as "program" or "exhibit" birds. The oldest resident is a twenty-five-year-old turkey vulture, trained as a program bird to maintain its dignity and composure perched on the heavily gloved lower arm of a staffer or volunteer. The handler, in turn, has been trained to describe to visitors the reason the bird is at the center and its place in the wild when it lived there, and then answer any questions visitors may have. Exhibit birds,

Environmental educator Hannah Putnam describes the habitat and habits of a Harris Hawk to a VINS audience. Hannah's work with program birds embraces a number of birds and audience levels.

largely untrainable for various reasons—and also injured or otherwise unable to return to their natural habitats—are kept in large enclosed settings designed to approximate their environment in the wild as closely as practicable. When possible, they are hooked up with roommates of their own species.

Education is a strong VINS component, as evident in VINS marketing director Molly Hutchins's description of the curriculum on our tour of the center. "We put on a week-by-week day nature camp here in Quechee; at our Manchester, Vermont, site; and in Hanover, New Hampshire. Five hundred and twenty-five kids went through our camp program this summer, quadruple what it was last year." Twice a day educators conduct half-hour programs that tell kids about whatever program bird is assisting in that particular demonstration. "The other two times a day," says Molly, "kids are taken on one of a number of nature hikes over the 3 miles of trails we have here in Quechee. There are four completely different programs every day."

Other regularly scheduled programs for groups of ten or more focus on nature walks and demonstrations of a wide variety of topics, from exploring natural habitats of Vermont to learning about the intricacies of bird flight. All are designed to enhance environmental learning and citizenship. Look for details about this, as well as an intriguing Citizen Science program involving more than 1,000 volunteer citizen scientists, on the comprehensive VINS Web site, listed below.

VINS's outreach program for the schools similarly includes natural history and environmental science. "The introduction to these topics to preschoolers in camp sessions is presented more comprehensively in the programs available to schools, either in workshops at the center, or by educators who go into the schools of Vermont and New Hampshire." Molly Hutchins continues, "In addition, we have just started a program offering teacher development workshops, where we teach teachers to teach the natural sciences. This assistance is offered pre-K through the twelfth grade."

Directions: The VINS Nature Center is located 1/4 mile west of the Quechee Gorge on the right-hand side of U.S. Route 4. From I-89, take exit 1 to U.S. Route 4 West. VINS is open to the public from May 1 through October 31, 10:00 a.m–5:00 p.m., seven days a week; and from November 1 through April 30, 10:00 a.m–4:00 p.m., Wednesday–Sunday. Admission is $9 for adults, $8 for seniors, and $7 for youth three to eighteen, with children two and under free. For more information visit www.vinsweb.org or call (802) 359-5000.

## How the Simpsons Chose Vermont as Home

Springfield

Here was the competition: Oregon, Illinois, Massachusetts, Colorado, Nebraska, Missouri, Louisiana, Florida, New Jersey, Michigan, Ohio, Kentucky, and Tennessee. Illinois was a close second; Florida was last. Vermont got the job done.

What made the difference? Each entrant submitted a three- to five-minute film, showcasing its community's "Simpsons Spirit." Twentieth Century–Fox provided interested parties with key filmmaking tools, including a digital video camera, *The Simpsons Movie* posters, and enough "Simpson-yellow" paint to last Homer through several nuclear meltdowns.

We'll let you judge each entry for yourself, but first we need to talk about the woeful disadvantage that Springfield, Vermont, had to overcome. Why would the ultimate winner not even have been *invited* to compete originally? That's right. Our Springfield people found out at the eleventh hour and weren't even able to start production on their video until two weeks before the deadline. Yes, outrage, one more time.

Well, whoever the perpetrators were, it didn't work! Yeah, baby, we came sailin' through. Final score: Vermont 1; Tennessee, Ohio, Oregon, and everybody else 0. In a futile attempt to prove that Hollywood has a heart, each of the other thirteen Springfields had a screening of

Photo courtesy W. J. Olender

**Simpsons creator and executive producer Matt Groening poses in Springfield with his creations at the premiere of *The Simpsons Movie*—his other reason to visit Vermont in 2007.**

their own, the night before *The Simpsons Movie* hit theaters nationwide late in July of 2007. And lest you think otherwise, this big-screen premiere was the real reason for all this folderol in the first place. To see the thirteen competing Springfield videos, go to: www.usatoday .com/life/movies/simpsons-contest.htm.

Directions: Just about anyone in Springfield will be happy to answer your Simpson questions, or anything else about the town. Just ask. Take I-91 exit 7 west into town on Route 11.

## Vermont's Fifteen-Year War against Billboards

Weston

To learn how Vermont became the first state in the nation to ban bill-boards, a good  place to start is the Orton family dining room table, back in the 1950s. Vrest Orton, a writer, activist, and founder of the Vermont Country Store chain (two stores), was passionate about the quality of his state's future, and frequently shared these opinions with his family.

"Yes, my father was one of the early supporters of getting rid of billboards in Vermont," says Lyman Orton, Vrest's son. In supporting this position over the years, Vrest Orton did not endear himself to the powerful outdoor advertising industry, who predicted that eliminating billboards would be the end of business as they knew it.  "About the same thing they said when we made bottles and cans returnable," says Lyman.

Orton went off to Middlebury College in the fall of 1959 with a strong recollection of those hours spent at the dinner table. At the same time, a phenomenon arrived to crystalize the pro- and anti-billboard debate.

"Have you heard of Seashell City?" Lyman asks. I hadn't. "Sea-shell City was a couple of nondescript buildings painted bright red on Route 7 between Brandon and Leicester—ten or fifteen miles south of Middlebury. They sold seashells . . . in the middle of Vermont! A few months after the buildings appeared, about fifty billboards went up—seemingly all the way from Massachusetts to Canada—on both sides of the road and painted bright red with white letters. They were just huge and went up so quickly they seemed to have grown out of the ground. When you went in the buildings, there were just these baskets full of seashells and other little knickknacks. Underwhelming, at best."

Seashell City helped provide a focus for the outrage on billboards, though, and what could happen all over the state unless something was done about it. As a college student who had listened well to his father and shared his taste for activism, Lyman acted.

"I rounded up a few fraternity brothers, and we went out late at night and began cutting the billboards down. We started with axes, but the support timbers seemed as big telephone poles, so we knew that wouldn't work. We bought crosscut saws, and over a couple of years we got rid of quite a few of them. It made the papers, of course, but we never got caught. (I guess the statute of limitations is up, so it's safe to tell this story!)"

Enter Ted Riehle, a Vermont legislator who took on the outdoor advertising lobby and a few of its business allies head-on. "He was the legislative hero for this issue," says Lyman. "I remember him visiting my father at our store a couple of times." In 1967, Riehle introduced legislation to ban all billboards except for small signs advertising local businesses and agricultural products—as well as to tear down all existing billboards. With the support of garden clubs throughout the state and other anti-billboard merchants, Governor Phil Hoff signed the bill into law in 1968. In 1974, Vermont felled its last billboard.

These days, Lyman limits his anti-billboard activism to board membership of Scenic America, which he calls "a small band of brothers and sisters born out of the Lady Bird Johnson–inspired Highway Beautification Act." Since then, says Orton, "that act has been amended so many times it could be called 'The Highway Desecration Act.'" Scenic America is the watchdog against the billboard industry, whose goal is to overturn or weaken anti-billboard legislation at federal, state, and local levels. So far so good. Forty years and counting.

To learn more about the Orton family and their activities, visit: www.orton.org; www.scenicamerica.org; and www.vermontcountry store.com.

## Mount Ascutney—New England's Premier Hang Gliding Mountain
### Windsor

Ever wonder what it would feel like to launch yourself off a 3,150-foot mountain (more than twice as high as Chicago's mam-

moth Sears Tower)? You could ask one of the ten to thirty hang
gliding pilots who take off from either the South or West Peak
launching site on Mount Ascutney every reasonably nice day. Or you
could take a tandem flight with a licensed pilot. All depends on your
level of interest.

If you just want to watch, you can either drive up or hike. The
drive is a wandering path of switchbacks beginning at the entrance
to Mount Ascutney State Park, and through the forest to the upper
parking lot, at 2,800 feet. (The launching sites are just 50 feet
higher, but a network of hiking trails will take you directly to the
summit, another 350 feet higher.) The trails to both launching sites
are well marked.

In times of need, some step forward. On this day, the author was
called on as crew chief when no one else volunteered. To everyone's
surprise, the pilot launched without mishap.

Take the trail at the far northwest side of the parking lot, and go left at the first fork. (The right fork goes to the lookout tower at the top of the mountain.) Continue until you come to a clearing, which is the West Peak launching site. On all but the calmest days, a wire crew of two (one on each wing) or three (another at the nose in rougher weather) is needed to assist with the launches.

Early or late in the day, when not enough experienced pilots are waiting to handle wire-crew duties, bystanders are asked to help out. Listen carefully to instructions if you volunteer for the wire crew, because the pilot's life could be in your hands. (Trusting lot, those hang glider pilots—in addition to being plucky.)

Tom Lanning is one of very few hang-gliding pilots to make it non-stop from Mt. Ascutney to the New Hampshire shore, 93 miles away. Here is an excerpt from his account of the four-hour trip, printed in the Vermont Hang Gliding Association newsletter:

"Although we battled black flies, soggy ground, and a brisk cross-wind on launch, we were soon airborne and soaring nicely in a WNW wind I measured at 25 mph. . . . As I topped out over 6,000 feet, I could finally see I-89, Concord, and Manchester [New Hampshire]. I decided to work across a cloud-bridge, and was rewarded with an easy 14-mile ride.

"Finally I saw the coast in the distance and started working on a plan to land on the beach. As I crossed Hampton Beach I gained a couple of hundred feet. I flew to the water's edge and down the coastline. As I flew back up the beach people were waving and shouting at me, and I waved back. I returned to the south end, did a number of slow "S" turns and floated onto the shore with a no-step landing.

"A crowd soon formed around me, and I answered the usual array of questions. After calling home, I broke down my glider, and was surprised at how quickly my friends Dan and Greg arrived to pick me up. After high-fives we loaded up and headed to a restaurant for clams, lobster, and steamers on an outside deck and watched the sun set. What a great ending to a great day."

Camping, hiking, and cross-country skiing are also among the attractions at Mount Ascutney, which is Vermont's only monadnock, meaning in this instance not part of the Green Mountains.

Directions: From Interstate 91 (exit 8), go .2 miles east on Route 131 to the stoplight; turn left on U.S. Route 5, traveling for 1.2 miles, and then bear left on Route 44A for 1 mile. Fans of *Death Wish* 1–5 may pay their respects to Charles Bronson at his grave site in the Brownsville Cemetery at the foot of Mount Ascutney. For more information go to www.vtstateparks.com/htm/ascutney.cfm.

## World's Longest Two-Span Covered Bridge

Windsor

Every bridge between Vermont and New Hampshire on the Connecticut River is owned by the State of New Hampshire.

Who said life was fair?

Back in 1764, King George III whimsically handed over Vermont to both New Hampshire and New York. (This is one reason Vermont seceded from the colonies in the first place.) New Hampshire wound up with the Connecticut River, all the way to the low-water mark on the west bank. For some reason Vermont and New Hampshire couldn't agree that the boundary should be in the middle of the river, as other states have been able to when haggling about river ownership. New Hampshire stubbornly insisted on the whole megillah.

Those decisions in the 1700s were made before dams were built on the river. Today, the boundary between Vermont and New Hampshire actually extends as much as a third of the way across the river, because the dams have flooded the valleys. This has been a sore point for many Vermonters ever since, particularly after a Supreme Court decision in 1934 validated King George's decision.

The Windsor-Cornish Bridge—or as New Hampshirites would have it, the Cornish-Windsor Bridge—is, at 449.4 feet, the longest wooden bridge in the country and the longest two-span wooden bridge in the world. Ed Varna, in *Covered Bridges of Vermont*,

★ ★ ★ ★ ★ ★ ★ ★ ★ ★ ★ ★ ★ ★ ★ ★ ★ ★ ★ ★ ★ ★ ★ ★ ★ ★ ★ ★ ★ ★

delivers his own double zinger in the direction of his cross-river neighbors: "This must be a treacherous location, since there were three previous bridges at this crossing of the Connecticut River, all destroyed by floods. . . . The bridge underwent major restoration work during the late 1980s, with neighboring New Hampshire footing most of the $4.65 million bill."

Ouch. And ouch.

You have to wonder, though: If Vermonters can put in and take out river craft on either bank, if Vermont fishing licenses include all of the Connecticut River, and if New Hampshire pays for bistate bridge repair, who was the real winner?

Directions: To reach the Windsor-Cornish Bridge, take I-91 exit 8 (from the south) or exit 9 (from the north). From Main Street (U.S.

**Here stands nearly 450 feet of living history. Windsor, Vermont, is part of its name, but the bridge itself belongs to New Hampshire. The beauty part . . . there's no downside!**

Route 5) at the south end of Windsor Village, turn onto Bridge Street just south of the stoplight. For more information and pictures visit www.coveredbridgesite.com/nh/cornish_windsor.html.

## Birth of the Vermont Nation
Windsor

The first constitution of the "Free and Independent State of Vermont" was adopted on July 8, 1777, less than a year after the signing of the Declaration of Independence, at Elijah West's Tavern, in Windsor. The present state of Vermont was occupied by New Hampshire, New York, and Massachusetts for much of the eighteenth century. These were not benevolent neighbors. Vermont residents fumed at the large fees New York laid on them just for transferring title to their lands, for example.

For this and other reasons, they decided to form their own republic and wrote a constitution modeled after Benjamin Franklin's for the State of Pennsylvania. The Vermont framers went further, however. Their constitution was the first to prohibit slavery, and the first to grant voting rights without regard to property ownership or specific income.

At about the time the Constitution was being finalized, British forces attacked and captured the fort complex of Ticonderoga, just across Lake Champlain. The British pursued the retreating American forces and met General Arthur St. Clair's rearguard at Hubbardton on July 7. Even though 1,000 Americans, including Ethan Allen and a band of 200 Green Mountain Men, successfully delayed the British advance, many residents on the west side of the Green Mountains had to run for their lives. Word of these alarming events reached Windsor on July 8, and the constitution was voted on—accompanied by a violent thunderstorm—just before the convention disbanded.

Vermont's Old Constitution House is a restoration of Elijah West's Tavern, which was located nearby. The land for the new location was

donated by the family of William Evarts, who served as secretary of state for President Rutherford B. Hayes and was chief counsel for the defense in the impeachment trial of President Andrew Johnson.

Directions: It is located at 16 Main Street at the northern end of the village of Windsor on U.S. Route 5, accessible from exits 8 and 9 on I-91. The museum is open to the public 11:00 a.m. to 5:00 p.m. on Saturday and Sunday from late May through mid-October. For more information call (802) 672-3773 or visit www.historicvermont .org/constitution.

In Windsor in 1777, delegates of the new Republic of Vermont drafted a constitution even more progressive than the U.S. Constitution signed ten years later in Philadelphia.

# First Ski Tow in America

In January 1934, the first ski tow in the United States was set up on Clinton Gilbert's farm in Woodstock. This simple rope tow, powered by a Model T Ford engine, helped begin Vermont's far-reaching ski industry and gave the sport a much-needed lift.

"When the rope tow started at Woodstock," says Charlie Asenowich, Vermont's first and most durable ski bum, "we teenagers at school got excited about skiing. Shortly thereafter, ski areas began cropping up like mushrooms."

# 5

## West Central

**I don't know** if I should be spreading this around, but there's a town here where, under special circumstances, you can get married for free! And they'll throw in a prenup and free tooth cleaning for the lucky couple. Of course there's a catch, but if you meet all the qualifications—number one that you're single—you might just be able to make it happen. (By the way, for the winners there's a lovely 16-ton, 20-foot-tall gorilla at the edge of town to help occupy a few of those awkward pre-honeymoon moments.)

In Proctor is a thirty-two-room, thirteen-fireplace, brick castle in the Flemish style, on the outside. But inside you'll discover a mixture of Queen Anne, Scottish baronial, Dutch neorenaissance, and Romanesque revival styles. (Head spinning yet?) This is the Wilson Castle, named for the owner. The builder sold it at auction after the death of his wife, whose millions provided the original financing. Mrs. Johnson (the wife), for her investment, insisted that all the bricks be imported from England. It was her money, after all. And she was English, after all. Guide Levi Nelson will cheerfully discuss the castle's spirit presence to the extent of your interest.

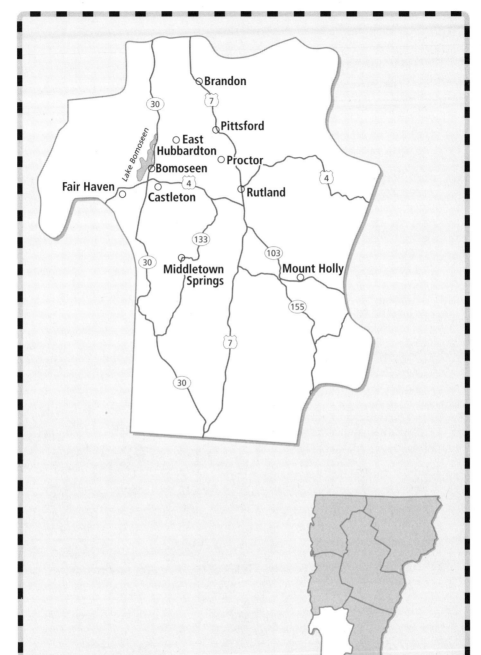

**Brandon**
30
7

**Pittsford**

Lake Bomoseen

**East
Hubbardton**
**Proctor**
**Bomoseen**

4

**Fair Haven**
**Rutland**
4

**Castleton**

133

**Middletown
Springs**
103
**Mount Holly**
30

155

7

30

★ ★ ★ ★ ★ ★ ★ ★ ★ ★ ★ ★ ★ ★ ★ ★ ★ ★ ★ ★ ★ ★ ★ ★ ★ ★ ★ ★ ★

### Lake Bomoseen, a Harpo Marx Hideaway

Bomoseen

Neshobe Island, in the middle of Lake Bomoseen, was named in honor of an Abenaki Indian scout who helped Ethan Allen and his Green Mountain Boys find and defeat the New Yorkers at Fort Ticonderoga in 1775. As late as the early twentieth century, Abenaki Indians returned to Indian Point every summer, to camp near the island.

From the mid-1920s until the early 1940s, Neshobe Island was the summer and weekend home of writer and critic Alexander Woollcott. It was also the retreat of a number of his celebrity friends, including Dorothy Parker, Helen Hayes, Ethel Barrymore, Irving Berlin, and Teddy Roosevelt Jr., who landed his seaplane on the lake when he came up to Neshobe from New York.

Woollcott's good friend Harpo Marx spent many weekends there, describing its eight acres as having a "wonderful variety of terrain and vegetation: miniature meadows, hills, and cliffs; quarries and beaches; wildflowers, flowering vines and bushes; [and] maples and evergreens," all just a quarter mile from the mainland. Woollcott built a rambling stone house on a ridge overlooking the lake on all sides, which became his permanent home the last seven years of his life.

As Harpo writes in his autobiography, *Harpo Speaks*, "the natives, in true Vermont fashion, didn't

Photo credit Minnie/Marx Eagle/Cathy Emerling

**Harpo (aka Michael Romanoff) tries to catch the eye of future diners.**

★ ★ ★ ★ ★ ★ ★ ★ ★ ★ ★ ★ ★ ★ ★ ★ ★ ★ ★ ★ ★ ★ ★ ★ ★ ★

bother anybody who didn't bother them, but the tourists were a nosy bunch. . . . One day novelist Alice Duer Miller went for a walk and rushed back to report that a group of tourists had rowed over from the mainland and were having a [somewhat raucous] picnic on the beach.

"I volunteered to deal with the interlopers. I stripped off all my clothes, put on my red wig, smeared myself with mud, and went whooping and war dancing down to the shore, brandishing an axe. The tourists snatched up their things, threw them into the boat, and rowed away fast enough to have won a . . . regatta. That put an end to the snooping that season."

Directions: To reach Lake Bomoseen, take U.S. Route 4 west to exit 4, in Castleton. Turn right on Route 30 and then go 2 miles to Bomoseen. To get more information on the state park at Lake Bomoseen, visit www.vtstateparks.com/htm/bomoseen.cfm or call (802) 265-4242.

## With This Essay, I Thee Wed
Brandon

All you newlyweds out there have missed the boat. Sorry!

But those of you still single—as well as all parents of said singles—may save yourselves mucho nuptial bucks by reading the following few paragraphs.

Brandon, you should know, is a wedding hotbed. Of the one hundred best towns for what top wedding expert Kathryn Gabriel Loving calls a "weddingmoon," four Vermont towns are listed and Brandon—home of the Lilac Inn—made the cut.

Now here's how Brandon may make it all the way to the top of the "destination wedding" heap: After hearing of their award, Lilac Inn owners Doug and Shelly Sawyer thought of a way to consolidate the PR that had fallen their way. "Why don't we give away a wedding?"

They talked with Brandon Chamber of Commerce executive director Janet Mondlak, who ran it by the membership. By the time the contest was announced, thirty merchants were on board.

★ ★ ★ ★ ★ ★ ★ ★ ★ ★ ★ ★ ★ ★ ★ ★ ★ ★ ★ ★ ★ ★ ★ ★ ★ ★ ★ ★ ★

Participants were asked to write two essays of 500 words or less, one describing the perfect Vermont wedding, and another detailing why they should be selected. ("Make us laugh; make us cry. Tell us a tale of love or triumph.") From the time the contest opened October 1 until it closed February 14 (nice touch!), 120 official entries had arrived for the announced September 1 wedding date. Two couples blew their chance completely by complaining about the cost of the affair ($40,000+), even though they would pay nothing if they won. Duh. The hardship stories outnumbered most other categories. "There are a lot of cancer patients and survivors getting married," said Janet, "a lot of financially deprived people. We said, 'Make us cry,' and they sure did."

The upshot is that New Yorkers Kristin Petty and Dan Kelleher touched all the right notes in their essay and interviews, and had their dream wedding that September 1, including ceremony, food, and lodging for one hundred guests, rehearsal dinner, wedding cake, wedding gown, tux, flowers, and farewell brunch, everything except the alcohol. But hey, attorney Jeff Smith prepared the prenups gratis, and dentist Tom Coleman threw in a tooth cleaning and oral examination for the happy couple.

Janet Mondlak is noncommittal about a repeat performance. "It was a lot of work for a lot of people," she says. "And I'm sure all those small businesses don't want to give away their goods and services on a continuing basis."

True enough. But odds are that when the kinks are smoothed out and the media coverage has worked its magic, Brandon may have generated enough tourist and destination wedding dollars to justify perpetuating the nation's first annual, essay-driven, nuptial bash.

Directions: To get to the Lilac Inn at 53 Park Street, coming in off U.S. Route 7, make a turn onto Route 73 (Park Street). The inn is the seventh house on the right. Check out www.lilacinn.com for more information. Also check out www.brandon.org for general information about the town or specific information about what may be offered to couples dreaming of the perfect Vermont wedding.

# Queen Connie— Rebar and Concrete (16 Tons, 20 Feet Tall)

"A larger-than-life gorilla lofts a Volkswagen Beetle as though it were an Olympic torch." *Car and Driver* (January 1991)

Sculptor—T. J. Neill, 1984

Location: Pioneer Auto Sales, 2829 U.S. Route 7, Brandon, Vermont

First Prize: "Carchitectural Wonders," *Car and Driver,* January 1991

Runner-up: "Four Giant-Sized Human Legs Support a Compact Sedan" (Prague, Czechoslovakia)

Second runner-up: "A Yugo Plunges through the Roof of a Barn" (Littleton, Colorado)

★ ★ ★ ★ ★ ★ ★ ★ ★ ★ ★ ★ ★ ★ ★ ★ ★ ★ ★ ★ ★ ★ ★ ★ ★ ★ ★ ★ ★ ★

## Big Wind at Grandpa's Knob
Castleton

Things don't always go as well as they might in the business of iden-
tifying Vermont curiosities. For example, as we approached Castleton,
we were on the lookout for signs of a historic wind energy development project installed in 1941 at Grandpa's Knob: the first large-scale
electricity-producing windmill in the United States, and the world's
largest at the time. One thousand Central Vermont Public Service
Corporation customers were the first in the world to have their
homes and businesses powered by the wind. This was to be the pioneer program for a renewable energy industry that more than a half-
century later is still barely getting off the ground.

The site was a 1,976-foot mountaintop between West Rutland
and Castleton. General Electric, the American Bridge Company, and
the Budd Company, along with the Central Vermont Public Service
Corporation and others, were involved in this colossal effort. The turbine consisted of a 240-ton base, and two 75-foot-by-11-foot blades,
each weighing eight tons. The blades churned out electricity in up
to 70-mile-per-hour winds, handling gusts of up to 115 miles per
hour. When a main bearing failed in 1943, though, wind generation
ground to a halt. Repairing it in the heart of World War II was not a
priority, and its replacement took more than two years to manufac-
ture and install.

This is what I knew (rather than what I *should* have known) when I
walked into the Castleton town manager's office.

"Can you tell me how to get to Grandpa's Knob?" I asked admin-
istrative assistant Jill Potter.

"Well, yes," she said and hesitated. "What are you looking for,
specifically?"

I told her we wanted a photograph of the windmill used to bring
electricity to the Castleton area. Jill said there wasn't much up there
to see. "That site was razed in 1946," said town manager Jon Dodd,
who had just walked into the room.

It was then I learned that the subject of our photo shoot had not existed for more than sixty years. What I missed was that after the part had been installed on March 3, 1945, with no problem, it worked without incident until one of the blades snapped off on March 26, flying 700 feet down the mountain slope before coming to rest. Engineers expressed confidence that repairs would begin immediately. Wartime shortages made steel a luxury, however. This, plus the fact that at the time coal was 20 percent cheaper than wind-produced electricity, meant that a decision to dismantle the project was inevitable.

Still, in the end, the wind turbine on Grandpa's Knob was considered an engineering success and helped scientists understand the behavior of the wind. It also helped improve wind turbine technology and proved that wind could be used to generate electricity. One might ask why a new Grandpa's Knob windmill or two might not work even better with today's technology. GE? Budd Company? Central Vermont? Anybody?

Regardless, Town Manager Dodd was not going to let me get away with such shoddy research. "So good luck to you, Don Quixote," he said as we left. He paused. "You know, 'tilting at windmills'?"

"Yes, I hear what you're saying," I said. "No need to explain."

"You never know," said Jon.

Directions: Castleton is 11 miles west of Rutland on Route 4. If you're interested, Jill Potter in the Castleton town offices will be able to tell you where Grandpa's Knob is. I, on the other hand, may never know. If you can't make it to Castleton, go to www.revermont.org/october.htm for more information on the project.

### The Pivotal Battle of Hubbardton
East Hubbardton

Here's what led up to the Battle of Hubbardton: In 1775 General Benedict Arnold, Ethan Allen, and eighty Green Mountain Boys captured Fort Ticonderoga, across Lake Champlain in New York. A year later the Americans had strengthened the fort and expanded it to

Mount Independence, in Orwell, Vermont, by building a floating bridge across the lake.

In 1777, though, a massive force of British seasoned Regulars moved south from Canada to overwhelm both Fort Ticonderoga and Mount Independence. To save his troops, American general Arthur St. Clair ordered the vastly outnumbered Americans to withdraw to the southeast. While the main force continued on, a rearguard of 1,000 men dug in at Hubbardton to slow down the Redcoats and their German allies. This led to the only Revolutionary War battle fought entirely on Vermont soil.

Although classified as a loss for the American forces, the Battle of Hubbardton is best known for being the single conflict precipitating British defeat in the Revolutionary War.

Although technically the Battle of Hubbardton was considered an American defeat, it accomplished what it was intended to do. So many casualties were inflicted on the British that they finally gave up. It was partially because of this bold stand that British general John Burgoyne said of the people of Vermont: "They are the most active and most rebellious race on the continent."

The 255-acre historical site includes trails leading to various stages of the battle. A visitors' center houses a museum with period artifacts and a large fiber optic map and accompanying narration of the battle stages.

Directions: Take U.S. Route 4 east from Rutland to exit 4, and then go north 7 miles to East Hubbardton. The battle site is on the left at 5696 Monument Road. The site is open late May through mid-October, Thursday–Sunday, 9:30 a.m.–5:00 p.m. For a complete account of the Battle of Hubbardton or more information about the site, see: http://historicvermont.org/hubbardton/hubbardton.html or call (802) 759-2412.

## Matthew Lyon—Elected to Congress from Jail

Fair Haven

The village green plaque pictured here just hints at Matthew Lyon's remarkable life and his contributions to early Vermont. Here's a little bit more of the story.

After attending school and beginning to learn the printing trade in his native Ireland, Matthew Lyon had guts enough to sail to America as an indentured servant at the age of fifteen. He first worked on a farm in Woodbury, Connecticut, and then moved to Wallingford, Vermont, where he gained his independence. During the Revolution, Lyon was commissioned as a lieutenant with Ethan Allen and the Green Mountain Boys and helped capture Fort Ticonderoga.

Lyon became wealthy after the Revolutionary War by learning how to make paper from wood pulp. He founded the village of Fair Haven and created the *Fair Haven Gazette*, a weekly for which he served as both editor and publisher. The *Gazette* gave Lyon a chance to express his strong pro-Jefferson views at the expense of John Adams, whom he viewed as a monarchist.

Lyon's influence helped elect him to Congress in 1796, where he wielded even more influence, even if by somewhat unconventional methods. On one occasion he spit on Federalist congressman Roger Griswold for insults against him having to do with his anti-Adams position. Griswold attacked him with his cane, but Lyon was able to get to the House fireplace, where he grabbed a poker and gave Griswold a nasty pasting.

To clarify the plaque's wording (compressed because of limited space), Lyon was jailed for violating the Sedition Act, true. But that act was declared unconstitutional a year later.

In 1798 Lyon was convicted and sentenced to four months in jail for violating the Sedition Act, signed by President Adams and making it unlawful for an American to defame a president. Even so, he easily won reelection despite being in jail at voting time. A year later the Sedition Act was declared unconstitutional, and in 1800 Matthew Lyon was able to cast the deciding presidential vote for his hero, Thomas Jefferson, in a runoff after an electoral college deadlock.

Lyon, his wife, and twelve children then moved to Kentucky, where he successfully ran for Congress once more. When Lyon moved again to Arkansas, he failed to become a congressman from a third state, but not because he was not successful in his campaign. Actually, he was elected but died before he could take a seat there. What a man! What a life!

Directions: Fair Haven is 12 miles west of Rutland on U.S. Route 4. Take exit 2 south to get to the center of town. For more information please visit www.fairhavenvt.org.

## A Town Pieced Together
Middletown Springs

In *Vermont Place Names,* Esther Monroe Swift tells the story of how Middletown Springs was created by absorbing parts of the four towns enclosing it.

In 1784 fifty residents of surrounding towns Tinmouth, Wells, Poultney, and Ira petitioned the legislature to create a separate town, principally because "the mountains around them are so impracticable to pass, it is with great trouble and difficulty that they can meet with the town they belong to for public worship and town business." A committee met with the petitioners and their surveyor, John Spaulding. The report was favorable and the town was created. Spaulding did such a good job that he was allowed to name the town. Spaulding chose "Middletown," both because it was the name of the Connecticut town from which he came, and because the new town, carved from the corners of the four towns around it, became the "middle" town.

Much earlier, both Abenaki Indians and a few of the settlers were aware of mineral springs on the bank of the Poultney River. The water's benefits were said to include the cure of rickets, scurvy, ulcers, and impotence. As testimony to the water's effectiveness with impotence alone, Rutland's Edna Faith Connell wrote in a 1939 issue of *The Vermonter* that "in 1797 there were eight families living [in Rutland County], having a total of 113 children. . . . Not one of the eight men ever had but one wife, and there was only one pair of twins in the lot, and only sixteen years difference between the first born of all the families."

Lee Dana Goodman, in *Vermont Saints and Sinners*, writes that the famous waters of Middletown's springs were bottled and sold by grocery stores and drugstores until the waters disappeared in the aftermath of the 1811 flood. Yet fifty-seven years later the springs miraculously reappeared—five of them, all with different chemical properties—and the bottling began again. The town was renamed Middletown Springs in 1884. But it was too late. A wave of skepticism about the water's curative powers doomed its future, and a grand hotel, the Montvert, built to accommodate the trade, was razed in 1906.

Directions: To reach Middletown Springs from Rutland, take Business Route 4 to West Rutland, and turn left on Route 133. Middletown Springs is 11 miles south.

### Giant Elephants . . . Once Roamed . . . in Vermont. Yes!
Mount Holly

Well, "giant" in the sense that they weighed twice as much as elephants living today and stood about 12-feet tall on all fours. Depending on whose opinion you accept, the woolly mammoth began grazing about 11,000 years ago, several thousand years after the ice retreated and grasslands reestablished themselves in the meadows of what is now Vermont. These large mammals chewed grass and leaves with eight-pound molars. These were low-tech tools that yielded high-volume greens mastication. They were essential, though. It takes a heap o' fuel to keep a five-ton woolly mammoth happy—or ambulatory, at the very least.

Fossil finds greatly aided late paleontologists in establishing written history.

★ ★ ★ ★ ★ ★ ★ ★ ★ ★ ★ ★ ★ ★ ★ ★ ★ ★ ★ ★ ★ ★ ★ ★ ★ ★ ★ ★ ★ ★ ★ ★ ★ ★ ★

A Swiss zoologist named Louis Agassiz proved to be instrumental in our understanding of what life was like in the Ice Age, among other things. In 1848, two years after he came to the United States—Harvard professorship in hand—Agassiz received tangible validation of a part of his theory. Workmen in Mount Holly, building a railroad from Bellows Falls to Rutland, uncovered the remains of a woolly mammoth from what were the mud layers of an ancient swamp, 11 feet below the surface. Most of the bones were taken by the workmen, but, as written in the *Vermont Semi-Weekly Record* in September 5, 1865, "the most perfect tusk was secured by Prof. Zadock Thompson and is lodged in the State Cabinet at Montpelier. This tusk was 80 inches long and four inches in diameter. The molar tooth, now in the possession of Prof. Agassiz, weighs eight pounds and presents a grinding surface of eight inches long and four broad. A plaster cast of it is on exhibition with the tusk at our State Cabinet."

Seventeen years later, near Brattleboro about 30 miles to the south, laborer James Morse was similarly mucking about on Daniel Pratt's farm and found the tusk of a young mammoth, about half the size of the Mount Holly specimen. The *Vermont Semi-Weekly Record* duly recorded this event as well: "The workman on discovering it took a piece to Mr. Pratt, remarking as he handed it to him, that he had found a curious piece of wood. Mr. Pratt on looking at it discovered its true nature." Thank you, Messrs Morse and Pratt.

Directions: The fossil tusk of the young woolly mammoth can be seen on the third floor of the Brooks Memorial Library (near the elevator), at 324 Main Street, Brattleboro. Call (802) 254-5290 or visit www.brooks.lib.vt.us for more information. A plaster cast of the full-sized mammoth molar can be seen at the Perkins Geology Museum, University of Vermont, 180 Colchester Avenue, Burlington. Call (802) 656-8694 or visit www.uvm.edu/perkins for additional information. (What happened to the original tusk is a mystery.)

★ ★ ★ ★ ★ ★ ★ ★ ★ ★ ★ ★ ★ ★ ★ ★ ★ ★ ★ ★ ★ ★ ★ ★ ★ ★ ★ ★ ★ ★ ★ ★ ★ ★ ★

### Horatio "Good Roads" Earle
Mount Holly

It wasn't President Eisenhower, as many think, who originated our federal highway system although he did sign the legislation. More than a half-century earlier, even before Henry Ford's first Model A rolled off the assembly line, Horatio Sawyer Earle proposed that the federal government create an interstate highway system.

Horatio Earle was born on a farm in Mount Holly in 1855 and became a traveling salesman for farm equipment at age thirty-one after working at a series of jobs. In 1889 Horatio and his wife and two sons moved to Detroit, Michigan. Eleven years later, Earle was elected to the Michigan Senate and became its first highway commissioner. His administration declared war on the "mighty monarch mud, which rules the road to the exclusion of everyone else." This led to the world's first mile of concrete road, paved in 1909 on Woodward Avenue in Detroit.

Earle envisioned a system of roads that would connect every major city and every state capital. He founded a group, the American Road Makers, and proposed that the federal government create an interstate highway system in 1902 (and yes, this bears repeating), *a year before* Henry Ford's first Model A rolled off the assembly line. Today that system has a total length of nearly 50,000 miles.

### Exploring the Sweetest Museum in New England
Pittsford

Attention out-of-state visitors: You've probably figured this out for yourselves, but unless your Vermont excursion includes late February (in southern Vermont) to early April (in northern Vermont), the closest you'll likely get to watching the production of syrup is the New England Maple Museum.

The first exhibit starts with a disclaimer: "Maple is the best known of America's oldest agricultural commodities, yet it probably is the most misunderstood."

Helped along by Mr. Doolittle, an animatronic host, visitors can see sugaring re-creations, from the days when American Indians first cut a diagonal gash in a tree and collected the sap as it flowed, to today's networks of plastic pipelines, and everything in between.

**Ever been lectured to by an animatron? You will be when you visit the New England Maple Museum.**

Directions: On U.S. Route 7, go north through Pittsford, and the museum is just outside town on the right. Hours vary by time of year. For more information visit www.maplemuseum.com or call (802) 483-9414.

## Wilson Castle

Proctor

Visitors come from all over the globe. "Guests from France said they had never seen anything like this—*in France,*" says tour guide Levi Nelson of Wilson Castle. What they see is a thirty-two-room, thirteen-fireplace brick structure built in the manner of a Flemish castle, with many arches breaking up the overall straight lines, but designed in a mix of architectural styles, to give the original owner the illusion of visiting a different country when leaving one room and entering

★ ★ ★ ★ ★ ★ ★ ★ ★ ★ ★ ★ ★ ★ ★ ★ ★ ★ ★ ★ ★ ★ ★ ★ ★ ★ ★ ★ ★

another. Queen Anne, Scottish baronial, Dutch neorenaissance, and Romanesque revival—they're all here.

Vermont-born Dr. John Johnson convinced his English bride to fund the castle's construction (and he's not available to tell us just how he got away with that), completed in 1874 at a cost of $1.3 million. Mrs. Johnson insisted that all the brick be imported from England, which today is causing a few structural problems because of the slightly warmer climate for which the brick was fabricated. When Mrs. Johnson died a few years after the castle's completion, it was repossessed and sold. In 1939 radio pioneer Herbert Wilson bought the 115-acre estate and created another radio station on the property. (The 100-foot tower still stands, although I found no bandwidth trace of the "still operating" WEWE-AM.) Wilson joined the Signal Corps in World War II and retired a colonel. He died in 1981 and left the estate to his daughter, who manages it today with *her* daughter.

Levi's favorite spot is the eight-sided music room, containing some of the castle's eighty-six stained glass windows, a beautiful fireplace, and an organ. About a third of the way up the wall is a French cherry

One classy destination at Wilson Castle is the French Renaissance Room. The round window you see is hand-painted; on the table is a statue of the moon goddess Helena.

wainscoting, above which is what looks like wallpaper but is actually a complex, hand-stenciled design, identical to that of the ceiling, which, we are told, took four and a half years to complete.

The Johnsons, and for the first couple of years the Wilsons, maintained an aviary, including a flock of peacocks that roamed the property. But the harsh Vermont winters and the ample local population of foxes, obviously finding the peacocks extremely tasty, made this a short-lived conceit.

Levi can remember just three times in his four years on the job that the Wilson—or could be Johnson—spirits came to call. "The first was about two years ago. When I came in one morning, a picture of Mr. Wilson's great-grandfather was lying over here about 20 feet from the fireplace. It was faceup, and the glass that had been in the frame was shattered in a perfect circle around it. I never found an explanation. I was the last person to leave, and the first to arrive next morning.

"Another one was a week ago today. I came in—the first to arrive—and upstairs there was a light on that I remember very specifically turning off. And again I was the last to leave the day before. I looked around and am sure that all the windows were shut and locked.

"The third occurrence was about the third week of the season last year. I came in—the first to arrive, but I'm not sure if I was the last to leave the night before—and in the same guest room in which the light was on the previous week, I went to open one of the doors so I could turn on a light, and the door opened before I could touch it. There were no windows open, so it couldn't have been the wind pushing it open. I suppose it could have been something related to the house settling, but I've never had any specific explanation for that, either."

Levi's guess is that the spirits, if there are any, are for the most part friendly. "No actions seem to have been directed toward me. Even the shattered photograph occurred while I was away from the castle. I like my job here, so until I see my name written on the wall in blood, I don't think I'll need to take a day off."

★ ★ ★ ★ ★ ★ ★ ★ ★ ★ ★ ★ ★ ★ ★ ★ ★ ★ ★ ★ ★ ★ ★ ★ ★ ★ ★ ★ ★

Directions: Off the Rutland Bypass, U.S. Route 4, take exit 6. Turn left 2 1/2 miles from West Rutland on West Proctor Road. Tours run daily from late May until late October, 9:00 a.m. to 6:00 p.m., the last tour starting at 5:30 p.m. For more information visit www.wilson castle.com or call (802) 773-3284.

## Bill Could Use a Little Help

Proctor

Going through the Hall of Presidents exhibit at the Vermont Marble Museum, it's hard not to notice that the two walls of bas-reliefs end with President George H. W. Bush. The two presidents succeeding him are missing. Is this a matter of laxity, or could this be a political statement of some kind?

That's completed plaster Bill on the left, and marble Bill-to-be on the right. If the museum doesn't find money enough to finish the job, the two may look like this for a long time.

I'm not sure. But let's take matters in sequence. Around 1995 or so, according to Proctor sculptor Brent Wilson, he was asked to add President Bill Clinton to the second row during that president's first term. But the museum wasn't able to meet his asking price, and the project was scrapped.

Fast forward to 2002. Local sculptor Vince Forte is commissioned to do a full bust of Clinton. Why a full bust? Well, the two side walls are full of presidents, and what remains is space for another row down the middle of the gallery. These will be three-dimensional busts instead of bas-reliefs, because they will be viewed from all sides rather than faces just protruding from marble slabs anchored to the wall.

Before he died in 2004, Forte had completed a plaster bust and was well into work on the final marble version. Again, Brent Wilson was asked to step into the breach. His preference would have been to sculpt a bas-relief, but alas, that decision had been set in stone. Wilson told Robert Pye, director of the museum, how much money he would require to finish the piece, but had not been given a go-ahead at this writing. "We need to get the money, because it is an expensive deal," Pye told the *Rutland Herald*.

About that time Bill Clinton was in the area, giving a commence-ment address at Middlebury College. Museum officials invited him to drop over to Proctor to take a look at the work in progress, but he was a no-show. Whether he was concerned about being hit up to cover some of the cost of completing his own bust is not known.

Making three phone calls to get permission for us to photograph the subject of this story, gift-shop associate Rob Hodge took us to the basement, opened a couple of locked doors, and removed several of layers of plastic wrap so we could see both Bill in the plaster-flesh and his marble twin-to-be. When finished, FYI, he will look jovial, with a slight gap between his two upper incisors.

Incidentally, both the Marble Museum men's room and ladies' room were 2007 finalists for the honor of "best bathroom in the

★ ★ ★ ★ ★ ★ ★ ★ ★ ★ ★ ★ ★ ★ ★ ★ ★ ★ ★ ★ ★ ★ ★ ★ ★ ★ ★ ★ ★ ★ ★

country." (Can you imagine how many judges that must have taken?) There were five finalists, with no clue as to the rankings from two to five, but hey, at worst, who wouldn't settle for having the fifth best bathroom in the country? (And if they each received a vote, this is about as good as the top prize.)

Directions: Once in Proctor, head west going over the marble bridge (you were expecting, maybe, prefabricated fiberboard?), past the Proctor library, and then turn north at the intersection. The museum is on the right. Said to be the largest of its kind in the world, the Vermont Marble Museum is open daily from mid-May until the end of October, 9:00 a.m. to 5:30 p.m. For more information visit www.vermont-marble.com or call (800) 427-1396.

### Who Cashed Social Security Check 00-000-001?
Rutland

When Ida May Fuller dropped by the Rutland Social Security office that November 4, 1939, morning, she knew she had been paying for something called social security for her three years of work as a teacher. "It wasn't that I expected anything, mind you," she said later. "I just knew that I had been paying for it and I wanted to ask the people in Rutland about it."

Ida May's claim was taken by claims clerk Elizabeth Corcoran Burke and transmitted to the Claims Division in Washington, D.C., for adjudication. The case was reviewed and sent to the Treasury Department for payment in January 1940. The claims were grouped in batches of 1,000 and a certification list for each batch was sent to the Treasury. Miss Fuller's claim was first on the certification list, so she was issued the first social security check: number 00-000-001, dated January 31, 1940, in the amount of $22.54. This was her first retirement check, which she received at age sixty-five. Over the next thirty-five years, until she died at age one hundred, Ida May received a total of $22,888.92 in social security benefits.

## John Deere, Forgotten Native Son

Rutland

The 5.2-acre John Deere Historic Site contains an archeological site, Deere's home, his blacksmith shop, and a gift shop. It is located in Grand Detour, Illinois. A plaque above the site of the shop in which John Deere apprenticed as a blacksmith stands in Middlebury, Vermont. But in Rutland, Vermont, the birthplace of John Deere, no statue, monument, or plaque exists to tell you so. The closest the town comes by way of commemoration is a copy of *John Deere's Company: A History of Deere & Company and Its Times*, donated to the Rutland Historical Society by a John Deere great-grand-something. It is not prominently displayed.

The steel plow revolutionized farming worldwide when John Deere first use cast steel, instead of iron, to turn the soil. The advantage: It cut through sticky soil without clogging.

This is not to say that the inventor of the steel plow, which revolutionized U.S. farming—and eventually worldwide farming as well—is not on the minds of Rutland residents. A local group is trying to raise

money for a bike path to be named after Deere but is having fund-ing difficulties. (It asked the John Deere Foundation for $120,000 but was turned down.)

It could be that Rutland has been slow coming on board with a public display of affection because John Deere didn't accomplish much before he left the state at age two. Illinois is reaping all of the rewards—both in fame and fortune—that Deere and his company had to bestow, because that's where the man spent most of his produc-tive years. Middlebury basks in a bit of reflected glory, because at least Deere learned the blacksmith trade there before moving on to greater things in the Prairie State. Yes, that would call for at least a plaque.

This has to hurt a little bit in Rutland. For all these years the ques-tion probably has been: "Why do we reward a resident who skipped town for good before he even went to school here?" and now it's "*How* do we reward a resident who skipped town for good before he even went to school here?" You can see the conflict in their minds. The same thing happened to Rudy Vallee. He left Island Pond when he was a toddler, and scant signs of his Vermont presence remain. The town of Sharon, on the other hand, has a statue to Joseph Smith, who brought Mormonism and the Angel Moroni to the world, and he was taken off to Palmyra, New York, before his first Vermont birthday. So it's a very tricky decision. We wish the citizens of Rutland well as they sort through the pros and cons.

# 6

# North Central

**Ever drive or** *walk across a floating, partially submerged bridge? We, as well as the residents of Brookfield, offer you that opportunity. Doesn't cost anything. And it's fun, though maybe a little scary the first time when your wheels sink down to the hubcaps. The lake is too deep for traditional pilings, we were told, so in 1820 they lashed logs together to get across after the ice melted. Each year water-soaked logs were replaced with new ones until 1884, when a bridge was built resting on tarred kerosene barrels that floated on the water. Today plastic containers filled with Styrofoam do the job.*

*Millions of people have seen* The Sound of Music *over the years— either the movie or the stage musical. Few know, though, that the Trapp Family Singers never sang "Do-Re-Mi," "Sixteen Going on Seventeen," or "My Favorite Things." Actually they sang very little in English, mostly in Italian and German. The movie songs were written by Richard Rodgers and Oscar Hammerstein for the actors who sang them.*

*Some ice cream flavors seem to be naturals. Others just don't quite make it. Ben & Jerry's, founded by two boys in Burlington, Vermont, back in 1978, push the envelope when it comes to flavor naming. The wackier the better. Do you remember Honey I'm Home, Economic Crunch, Sugar Plum, or Ethan Almond? Me either. The boys are good, but sometimes they try just a tad too hard at the naming game. For enough groan-inducing ice cream flavor puns to last you a lifetime, be sure to read the tombstones at the Flavor Graveyard in Waterbury.*

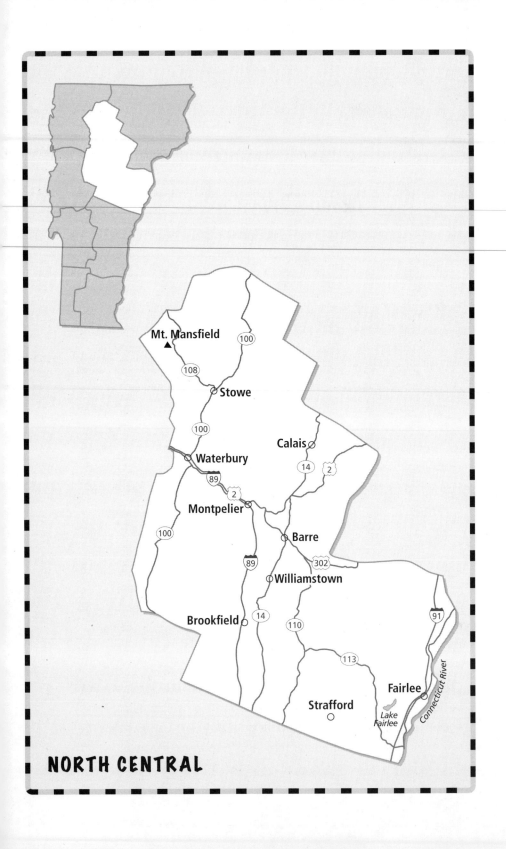

Mt. Mansfield
▲
100

108

Stowe

100

Calais

Waterbury

14    2

89

2

Montpelier

100

Barre

89

302

Williamstown

Brookfield    14

110

91

113

Fairlee

Strafford

Lake
Fairlee

Connecticut River

**NORTH CENTRAL**

## 5,000 Miles of Snowmobile Trails—That's VAST

Barre

Keep in mind this is a teeny state. So it's unusual enough for there to be nearly 5,000 miles of snowmobile trails crisscrossing its meadows, forests, mountains, and valleys. But Vermont is also the only New England state with interconnecting trails that not only provide access through one another, but also reach beyond the state's borders into Massachusetts, Quebec, New York, and New Hampshire. Seven customs entry points connect Vermont and Quebec trails alone.

Alexis Nowalk, trails administrator for VAST—the Vermont Association of Snowmobile Travelers—walks me through the various networks crucial to making all of this happen. "These trails are all maintained by the 138 local VAST clubs, which are responsible for all grooming, trail construction, and repair during the off-season. Each club has a contract with VAST to groom the trails twice a week during our sixteen-week season [December 16 to April 15], and we reimburse them for each mile groomed. The clubs send me a grooming log sheet weekly."

Growing up in Buffalo, New York, Alexis has been a snowmobiler since childhood, so no drastic lifestyle changes were necessary when she joined VAST in resources management, which led to a job in the U.S. Forest Service as a hydrologic technician and later as a GPS consultant mapping wetlands.

"Eight thousand private-property owners allow us on their land," says Alexis. "The relationships we maintain with them are key to our success. We try to keep communications open, and the clubs in turn host landowner appreciation dinners, stack wood, maybe give gifts, whatever seems appropriate." A few agencies that manage public lands provide access as well, such as the U.S. Forest Service, the Agency of Natural Resources, and the U.S. Fish and Wildlife Service.

Then there are the 27,000 members, whose registration and trail passes provide VAST with its principal sources of revenue. Several

★ ★ ★ ★ ★ ★ ★ ★ ★ ★ ★ ★ ★ ★ ★ ★ ★ ★ ★ ★ ★ ★ ★ ★ ★ ★

years ago, membership stood at a high of 42,000. Alexis believes, however, that two recent phenomena—warmer winters and mandatory liability insurance—have resulted in the falloff.

The most exciting project in work is the conversion of the 96-mile Lamoille Valley Rail Trail to a four-season multiuse recreation path. VAST recently signed a contract with the Vermont Agency of Transportation to manage the estimated ten-year, $7 million project, which will stretch through Franklin, Lamoille, and Caledonia Counties. "Senator Sanders was instrumental in securing a $5 million high-priority grant for this project through the Highway Administration," says Alexis. "We're very fortunate."

For more information about VAST or the trails it maintains, visit www.vtvast.org.

Photo courtesy VAST

**VAST's 27,000 members depend on 8,000 Vermont private property owners to allow snowmobilers to use their land—part of the 5,000 miles of trails to be enjoyed each winter.**

# Second-Generation Trailmaster

When Scott Fletcher was drafted into the Air Force in 1969, he gave his year-old Evinrude snowmobile to his parents and told them to keep it warm for him. By the time he returned home in 1973, Scott's parents had become avid snowmobilers. His dad had traded in the Evinrude for a new sled and was named trailmaster for the Rockingham Abenaki Snowmobile Club two years earlier. Scott had a lot of catching up to do.

Scott's parents, long-distance riders, once drove their snowmobiles up to their camp in Morgan, Vermont, north of Seymour Lake (the largest totally within the state's borders) near the Canadian border. This was a 240-mile, two-day drive, which included a motel stay in Randolph or thereabouts.

Today Scott is trailmaster for the Abenaki Club, and his grooming days go back to the early 1970s, when grooming devices were not as advanced as they are today. "We used to drag bedsprings—you name it," says Scott. He and his wife, Maureen, are looking forward to the day when they can regularly make the round-trip Scott's mother and father traveled years ago. "That's going to have to wait until I retire," says Scott, who has worked at the Grafton Cheese Company for forty-one years, and for thirty-five of them has been head cheese maker. "We'd like to make that trip now, but there's a bit too much traffic on the weekends, and we're too busy to go up in the middle of the week."

★ ★ ★ ★ ★ ★ ★ ★ ★ ★ ★ ★ ★ ★ ★ ★ ★ ★ ★ ★ ★ ★ ★ ★ ★ ★

### The E. L. Smith Quarry—A Dig of Uncommon Depth

Barre

Some call it Graniteville; others call it the Rock of Ages. But whatever you call it, this is one big hole. To be precise, at 600 feet deep it is the largest deep-hole granite quarry in the world. Marcelle Moran is senior among the guides who conduct narrated tours from the visitors' center to the quarry. With forty-six years on the job, she's senior by a sizable margin. Actually, Marcelle was director of the visitors' center for twenty years until she "retired" in 1995. Her handpicked successor, former teacher Todd Paton, is still on the job. "We see between 55,000 and 65,000 visitors each [six-month] season," she says.

Marcelle offers to take us on a personal tour of the quarry, just behind the shuttle bus pulling out of the parking lot. During an interim stop at the granite bowling alley (result: gutter ball), Marcelle says: "They thought they'd have a big turnaround with these granite bowling alleys, but the bowling balls couldn't take it!" Kids have fun trying it out, though.

We reach the fenced-off quarry itself moments later, as the narrator gets into her spiel: "Now if you see the derrick over here to our left, that little yellow cage it is transporting is called a rider box. That's where our men go in every day. They are lowered down and taken out at the bottom. Our derricks are all run electrically, and if you look about 50 yards behind each of them, you'll see a red building with white trim. That's where the derrick operator sits and runs the derricks. Now from where he is, it's impossible to see the bottom of the quarry. And from where we're standing, *we* can't see the bottom of the quarry either. So we have a signalman who will sit in or near that little red shack right on the edge of the quarry wall. He relays hand signals to the derrick operator, and that's how we run our derricks. Because of the loud noise from the drilling, we're unable to communicate with walkie-talkies. So everything is done through hand signals."

The number of people employed in the granite industry in and around Barre has shrunk to half the 3,000 who worked here in the mid- and late-twentieth century. The number of imported headstones from China and India increases by the year. Although the quality of the imported stones is poor, labor costs are so low in China that manufacturers can sell them for a fraction of the price paid for U.S.-made stones.

The visitors' center can do nothing about this, of course, but the company can add attractions to get visitor numbers back up where they once were. One popular new addition is a sandblasting activity that gives the user a chance to create his or her own design on a tile or trivet, blow the abrasive into the stencil, cut the design into it, and take it home for a fee.

Directions: Take exit 6 on Interstate 89. Follow Route 63 to the bottom of the hill. At the traffic light, follow the signs to Granite-ville/Graniteville Quarries. Go straight up Middle Hill Road. About 200 feet past Lazy Lion Campground will be the driveway for the Rock of Ages on the left at 558 Graniteville Road. The visitors' center hours vary by season. For more information visit www.rock ofages.com or call (802) 476-3119.

High-tech doesn't help in the quarry business, at least at the Rock of Ages. Because the drilling noise is so loud, walkie-talkies are useless. Hand signals are used exclusively.

## Help . . . the Bridge Is Sinking!

Brookfield

Plaque reads as follows:

> THE FIRST FLOATING BRIDGE AT THIS LOCATION WAS BUILT BY LUTHER ADAMS AND
> NEIGHBORS, IN 1820. THE PRESENT BRIDGE IS THE SEVENTH, AND WAS BUILT BY
> THE VERMONT AGENCY OF TRANSPORTATION DISTRICT 6, IN 1978.

In the early 1800s inhabitants of Brookfield could cross the ice in the winter, but they could not drive carriages over the pond in the summer. To drive around the pond took too much time. In 1820 the townspeople created a bridge of logs to connect the two sides. Each year water-soaked logs were replaced with new ones until 1884, when Orlando Ralph devised a bridge that rested on tarred kerosene barrels that floated on the water. In 1978 the wooden barrels were replaced with plastic containers filled with Styrofoam. The Sunset Lake Floating Bridge is supported by those floating barrels, we're told, because the lake is too deep for traditional pilings.

Well, okay . . . so you arrive at 8:00 a.m., for example. You're looking at that bronze plaque, just above you on the right. No traffic, either coming your way or behind you, to witness your cowardice. Ahead, you see what are probably the planks of a wooden bridge, but they're half a foot beneath the blackness of what could be a 500-foot-deep lake. Index finger ready to hit 911 on your mobile? Go for it!

Actually, the 150-yard-or-so voyage is painless and fun. You may even want to go back and forth a couple of times, traffic permitting. You can also fish off the bridge or swim near it, in addition to driving your car over it. Your tires will get wet, but the bridge will get you safely across. No trucks, though.

If you come by in January when the bridge is closed, you may be in time to catch the ice-cutting demonstration. See how ice was harvested on Sunset Lake in the nineteenth century, including the ice boom used to move blocks of ice to horse-drawn wagons. Lots of food, fun, and an ice-hauling contest. No admission.

For Brookfield residents, crossing the bridge is transportation. For everyone else, the first time is an adrenaline rush.

Directions: From I-89 South, take exit 4. On Route 66, go east 1 mile to Randolph Center, and turn north. One mile farther, where Route 66 makes a sharp right, go left onto Ridge Road. Drive 6 miles to Route 65, and turn left. Sunset Lake Bridge is 200 feet on the left. For more information see www.central-vt.com/web/floating.

## "A Folly"

Brookfield

So we have a sinking bridge over on the north side of town. And if you're returning to I-89 exit 4, you'll see a nautical curiosity of another kind on the south side of town. At the end of a dock across the road from the house at 408 Ridge Road is a Downeast lobster boat, serenely bobbing—or seemingly so—at the lowest of ebb tides: two acres of lawn.

*A Folly,* owned by Al Wilker and his wife, Vance Smith, wasn't always the name of the boat. Al was halfway into the refurbishing of *Caroline,* as the lobster boat was known back then, when their good friend Tommy Gillette died—"Much too early," says Vance. So before life passed them by, they chucked it all and bought a 36-foot sailboat. For the next few years they spent a lot of time tooling around Lake Champlain and then came back to decide what to do with *Caroline,* which had been sitting in the barn all that time.

*A Folly*, formerly the *Caroline,* is a memorial to Vance and Al's dear friend Tommy Gillette.

Then it came to them. First they built the dock. Then they towed *Caroline* across the street and down the hill. Then they renamed her *A Folly,* which perfectly matches the whimsical English definition often applied to formal gardens: "An architectural construction that isn't what it appears to be."

Says Vance, "It's a memorial to Tommy Gillette, to getting the most out of life when you can. And sometimes, in the right light and after a few beers, you can see whitecaps."

Directions: From the Brookfield Floating Bridge, drive south on Ridge Road a little less than 1 mile. *A Folly* is across the street from 408 Ridge Road.

★ ★ ★ ★ ★ ★ ★ ★ ★ ★ ★ ★ ★ ★ ★ ★ ★ ★ ★ ★ ★ ★ ★ ★ ★ ★ ★ ★ ★ ★ ★ ★ ★

## Morey's Steamboat—Was Fulton a Fraud?

Fairlee

Most history books credit Robert Fulton's *Clermont* with making
the first successful steamboat trip in 1807. True, Fulton's Hudson
River voyage from New York City to Albany was the first commercial
steamboat service in the world.

*Gould's History of River Navigation,* however, describes the voyage
not as a success, but as a disaster. "The rudder had so little power that
the vessel could hardly be managed. The spray from the wheels dashed
over the passengers." The skippers of other river craft took advantage of
the *Clermont*'s unwieldiness, and cut in front of her to save time.

As a result, the *Clermont* was completely rebuilt and tried again
the following May, with Fulton himself aboard. The voyage got off to
a bad start by leaving several passengers behind when the ship made
an uncharacteristic on-time departure. Even so, a leaky boiler was the
only problem on the upriver voyage. On the passage back down the

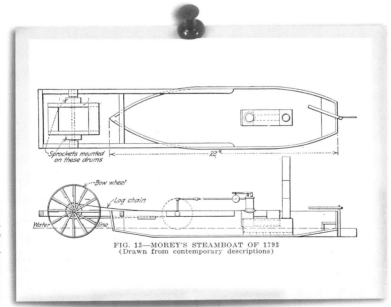

Photo courtesy Hagley Museum

FIG. 13—MOREY'S STEAMBOAT OF 1793
(Drawn from contemporary descriptions)

If Fulton started out so badly—poor design, bad planning, internal
bickering—why did he come off so well in the history books? Simple:
He managed to strike the best financial deal.

★ ★ ★ ★ ★ ★ ★ ★ ★ ★ ★ ★ ★ ★ ★ ★ ★ ★ ★ ★ ★ ★ ★ ★ ★ ★ ★ ★ ★

Hudson, though, there were more leaks. According to Gould, "After fifty-seven hours of struggling, the engine ceased to work." The boat grounded, with Captain Wesswell blaming the pilot and the pilot blaming the captain. This led "to a torrent of vituperation on each side, [as well as] blows, in which one of the parties was knocked down, and one received a black eye." Another successful voyage!

But here's the kicker: The *Clermont* was not the first, but the twelfth steamboat to be built and become a part of river traffic in the nineteenth century. Anachronism aside, today we might be calling this fiasco Fultongate.

In 1792, fifteen years earlier, Fairlee, Vermont, inventor Samuel Morey built a steamboat with a paddle-wheel in the prow. One Sunday he and an assistant, John Mann, made their first trip across the Connecticut River and back from Orford, New Hampshire, to Fairlee. A few years later, Morey constructed a new and improved version, with paddle-wheels on each side for more speed and better stability. He sailed from Bradenton, New Jersey, to Philadelphia on the Delaware River, where his newly christened *Aunt Sally* was publicly exhibited. Fulton and Morey were aware of each other's efforts as early as 1793, and the race was on for the funding that would assure commercial success.

Enter Robert R. Livingston, chancellor of New York State, a wealthy entrepreneur, and an inventor as well. Before meeting Fulton, Livingston took a ride in Morey's steamboat and offered to back him in a joint venture, but Morey refused when Livingston insisted on too large a percentage of the proceeds. Livingston then went to Fulton, and the deal that resulted is what eventually made its way into the history books. When Morey heard about it, he is said to have scuttled the *Aunt Sally* in what is now Lake Morey.

But Samuel Morey, holder of a number of patents, also designed and built the Bellows Falls Canal in 1802. (See Chapter 2). So it's not as though he brooded rudderless after getting the shaft from Fulton and Livingston.

Fairlee is located off Exit 15 on I-91 north; http://www.ctrivertravel.net/fairlee.htm.

Structure a self-guided tour of the most walkable town around, by time available, interests, or as your mood suggests. Plan your route on a downtown bench over a cup of coffee.

## Walking the Nation's Smallest Capital

Montpelier

Just a few miles south of exit 8 on I-89, the tableau of green valleys, farms, and hills spread out below make a highway warrior feel more like a Piper Cub pilot on the last approach before putting down. On your right is the city of Montpelier, home of fewer than 8,000 souls, with the population swelling to nearly 8,200 when the legislature is in session (representatives plus assistants, press, lobbyists, and assorted hangers-on). Just off the exit you can see the golden dome. Now there's proof you're in a capital city.

If the legislature isn't in session, you'll have a good shot at a parking spot near the capitol building. If so, walk in the front door and

take a tour if you'd like. When you're ready, walk out the other side to a trail that leads straight to 185-acre Hubbard Park. Here you'll find wooded stands of oak, beech, pine, and hemlock, dotted with picnic areas, a pond, hiking trails, and a 54-foot stone observation tower.

An alternative is to walk back out the capitol front door and left down State Street 1 block to the Vermont Historical Society Museum. After you browse a bit, ask one of the informed and accommodating docents the best way to spend the next couple of hours (or days) in the nation's smallest capital. Bring a map to check off likely destinations. She'll (there've been only ladies on duty the times I've visited) tell you where to pick up a four-color pictograph map of the downtown area (the one with the buildings labeled), so you can sit on a bench with a cup of coffee and plan a route tailored specifically to your interests, depending on the length of your stay.

Vermont's beautiful State House was the first commercial building to be constructed from Barre granite. (And that's real gold on the dome.)

Directions: For capitol tour information visit www.vtstatehouse.org or call (802) 828-0386; for more information about the smallest capital, visit www.montpelier-vt.org.

### The Morse Brothers, Cracker-Barrel Philosophers Extraordinaire

Montpelier

We'd heard about Burr Morse–his farm, his eight-generation maple sugaring operation, his farm store, his wit and wisdom. But when I told Burr about *Vermont Curiosities* and wanted to hear a couple of the stories that had made him famous, Burr backed off a bit.

"I've got a monthly column to write," he said. "My second book will be coming out soon." I had the feeling Burr needed that material for his own projects and was leery of diluting the franchise. He suggested I talk to his brother Elliott—"Just as good a storyteller," he said—who would be in on the day we were dropping by. Not having heard Burr in action, I can't make the comparison. We did enjoy the next hour, though.

⋆ ⋆ ⋆ ⋆ ⋆ ⋆ ⋆ ⋆ ⋆ ⋆ ⋆ ⋆ ⋆ ⋆ ⋆ ⋆ ⋆ ⋆ ⋆ ⋆ ⋆ ⋆ ⋆ ⋆ ⋆ ⋆ ⋆ ⋆ ⋆ ⋆ ⋆ ⋆ ⋆ ⋆ ⋆

Elliott greeted us in the cross-country ski warming room. (Ski trails are another Morse enterprise.) It was July and we were in no need of warming, but sat down to a great view of the mountains and meadows to the south. Elliott began with a historical introduction to his family, who got their American start in Calais, a few miles to the north. (Pronunciation time-out: "Calais" is pronounced CAL-us. . . . Get over it. Elsewhere in the state, "Berlin is pronounced BUR-lin; "Barre," BEAR-ee; "Leicester," LES-ter; and "Charlotte," shar-LOTT. . . . I said, get over it.)

Anyway, Elliott's great-great-great-great grandfather framed Calais's Old West Church in 1823. "It's exactly as it was then," says Elliott. "It's never had electricity, never had water or bathrooms. And we hope that never will change." He plunged directly into his Old West Church story.

**Rural, rustic, homespun—the Morse brothers sure measure up as classic "Cracker-Barrel" philosophers. They may not have a lot of time to give you, but take what little you can. Elliot sat down with us to chat.**

★ ★ ★ ★ ★ ★ ★ ★ ★ ★ ★ ★ ★ ★ ★ ★ ★ ★ ★ ★ ★ ★ ★ ★ ★ ★ ★ ★ ★ ★ ★ ★

"In 1843, there was this group across the country called Miller-ites, led by William Miller, who came from the New York shore of Lake Champlain." Disciples of Miller, a former U.S. Army captain and unordained minister, claimed to have discovered when Jesus Christ would return to earth, as stated in the Bible. "His mathematics told him the world would cease to exist on New Year's Eve, 1843," continues Elliott. Millerites were quite widespread across the country, and there was a large group in Calais.

"So that summer, of course, they didn't bother to put up any hay or food for the winter, because they thought they wouldn't need anything. In fact, a few gave away their farms, including their horses and cows. And on New Year's Eve, 1843, they went to the Old West Church, dressed in white Ascension robes. They put a grandfather's clock in front of the altar, and they waited. It was so crowded that some couldn't get in and just looked through the windows. They thought at the stroke of midnight it would all be over. . . . But it wasn't.

"So they waited a few minutes, and then quite dejectedly walked away—because of course they had no horses. And then the Reverend said: 'Well, I guess I made a small mistake.' So he set a date for the following year; and when the same thing happened, that was the end of it. Now, some of these people moved in with relatives. Others found shacks to live in, and that's where they ended their days.

"Well, they didn't string up Reverend Miller, but that religion disappeared, only to evolve into today's Seventh Day Adventists."

Elliott moves right along. "Then, there's the story of the human hibernation. It was a way people in my great-grandfather's day discovered to freeze older people for the winter—because there wasn't enough food for them—and then thaw them in April so they could help with the planting, as well as the fall harvest. . . ."

Sorry. Out of space. For that story, you're going to have to wait for the next edition of *Vermont Curiosities*—or hear it from Elliott yourself.

★ ★ ★ ★ ★ ★ ★ ★ ★ ★ ★ ★ ★ ★ ★ ★ ★ ★ ★ ★ ★ ★ ★ ★ ★ ★ ★ ★ ★

Morse Farm is 2.7 miles northeast of the State Capitol, on Main Street beyond the rotary and just past Center Road on the right. Calais is 10 miles north of Montpelier on Route 12. The Old West Church is in Calais on Old West Church Road, .8 mile south of its intersection with Kent Hill Rd; www.morsefarm.com.

## Who Sculpted Little Margaret?

Montpelier

Back in the northeast corner of Green Mount Cemetery is a granite gravestone statue of a girl of seven, Margaret Pitkin, or "Little Margaret," as she is called by the thousands of visitors worldwide who have stopped by since she died in 1900.

"The story goes that the Pitkin family commissioned a sculptor named Harry Bertoli to make a statue of their little girl, who had just died of spinal meningitis," says Green Mount director Patrick Healy. "But when Bertoli completed the work and presented his bill, the family said, 'No, we're not going to pay for this.' When the sculptor asked why, they said, 'Because one of her shoe buttons is missing.'" But Harry Bertoli had worked from a photograph he was given, and when the family told him he had not faithfully followed it,

**Why do thousands worldwide visit the grave of a girl dead more than 100 years?**

★ ★ ★ ★ ★ ★ ★ ★ ★ ★ ★ ★ ★ ★ ★ ★ ★ ★ ★ ★ ★ ★ ★ ★ ★ ★ ★

he pointed out the missing shoe button in the photo and was immediately paid in full.

"He [Bertoli] was my maternal grandfather," says Lynda Royce, of Montpelier. "He was born in Carrara, Italy, and was a graduate of the Carrara Academy of Art. When he was eighteen, he was commissioned to come to Vermont to teach sculpturing. My aunt Amelia, Harry's daughter, was the same age as Margaret. Harry used her arms to pose for the statue, because he didn't have enough to go on from the photo alone."

But wait! The history of this work then takes a strange twist. After the death of Harry Bertoli, Ettore Bonazzi, a former employee of Bertoli's, claimed full credit for sculpting Little Margaret. In subsequently published articles, including a 2002 *Vermont Sunday Magazine* story called "The Art of History," no mention is made of Bertoli, the implication being that Bonazzi alone negotiated with the Pitkins, both regarding the work to be done and the payment for it.

But did Bonazzi simply wait until his former employer was dead before "pulling a fast one"? Manuel Garcia, a grandson of Bertoli's, owns a photograph showing the model of Little Margaret in Harry Bertoli's statuary shop. Also shown in the photo are several employees, including Bonazzi. "This to me strongly indicates that my grandfather was commissioned to do the statue," says Manuel. "And also that he carved the stone—perhaps with the assistance of others—and negotiated on his own with Mr. Pitkin over the missing shoe button and final payment." At least as far as Manuel's concerned, this seems to put to rest the question of who carved Little Margaret.

Directions: Green Mount Cemetery is on the west side of Montpelier. From the center of town, take U.S. Route 2 (State Steet) west about 1 mile. For more information see www.montpelier-vt.org/cemetery/greenmount.cfm#map or contact Superintendent Patrick Healy at (802) 223-5352.

# Six Feet Under Is Only One Way to Go

Cemetery management in the twenty-first century is developing its own set of issues. "The baby boomers want options," says Montpelier's Green Mount Cemetery superintendent Patrick Healy. "They do not want to be told 'either it's this or it's nothing.' They'll go someplace else. So we're trying to go with the times.

"For one thing, there's much more cremation going on today. Up in an older part of the cemetery is a section that hasn't been used since we bought the place in 1854. It's all ledge [a shelf of rock] 6 inches below the surface. So what we do is sell plots about 3½ by 11 feet wide. We drill cores [Patrick shows me a copper/bronze casing about 3 feet long by 3 inches in diameter] the way rock is prepared before being blasted to carve out a freeway. We can put a monument there, because all you have to do is pour a little bit of concrete on the ledge itself, pin it, and when 'your time' comes, we just unscrew the cap on the casing, take a funnel, pour you in it—and you're home."

"But what if I'm claustrophobic?" I say.

"I haven't seen or heard a problem yet," says Patrick.

"We have another section called Woodland Gardens. It's not big, but there are some paths through the woods. It's not your traditional 'mow the lawn' area. What we found was that a lot of people were spreading their relatives' cremated remains out in nature—in the Atlantic Ocean, Florida, or a favorite fishing spot—but they still wanted a place to come and remember. The stones are flush to the ground, so nature is disrupted only slightly." Strange as it seems, cemeteries now are in competition and have to figure out how to market their services. "I'll probably be doing commercials on WDEV before long!" says Patrick.

★ ★ ★ ★ ★ ★ ★ ★ ★ ★ ★ ★ ★ ★ ★ ★ ★ ★ ★ ★ ★ ★ ★ ★ ★ ★ ★ ★

## A Touch of Swedish Lapland in Vermont

Stowe

The Kaffi Reykjavik Ice Bar, in Reykjavik, Iceland, gets its raw materials from Vatnajökull, the largest ice cap in Europe. The Icehotel in Swedish Lapland cuts ice blocks for its walls and bar stools from the frozen Torne River, 750 miles north of Stockholm. Fortunately, Rusty Nail Bar and Grill general manager Ken Walters found an ice furniture source in Pennsylvania for his Stowe, Vermont, establishment—the only frozen saloon in the Northeast, so far as he knows.

Ken's inspiration was Quebec's thirty-six-room Ice Hotel, but his objectives were considerably more modest: a congenial space for customers to cool down and share a cold (make that ice-cold) drink after

Photo courtesy Rusty Nail Bar

Since we last visited the Rusty Nail, the Ice Bar has seen hard times— but only temporarily, we hope. Last winter's warmth washed it out, but we're thinking it'll be back. Call first.

an afternoon on the slopes and ski trails. Even so, it takes twenty-two tons of ice every year to construct the Rusty Nail's 800-square-foot Ice Bar, including 8-foot walls, tall ice tables, and the 25-foot-long bar itself. The space has opened on Christmas week every year for the past three years and draws enthusiastic—and curious—traffic from more than 100 miles away.

Ice bartender Kate Wise has heard it all from tourists some might call skeptical; others, clueless:

"What is that bar *really* made of?"

"Is it the same temperature here as it is outside?"

"How do you keep an ice bar going in the summer?"

The last one is easy. "Come back in August and see," she says.

Even though Kate and the rest of the ice bartenders are outfitted with toasty jackets, hats, gloves, and boots to reduce the discomfort level, it isn't nearly as pleasant for them as wearing tee shirts while schmoozing with customers at 72 degrees—in August, for example, when that curious customer returns to learn the warm-weather fate of New England's only ice bar.

Directions: Take Route 108 (Mountain Road) out of Stowe, and the Rusty Nail Bar and Grill is located at 1190 Mountain Road. Open at 3:00 p.m. daily, weather permitting. Visit www.rustynailicebar.com or call (802) 253-6245 for more information.

## Maria von Trapp—A Lifetime of Service

Stowe

She is not eager to talk about herself. "Read the book," she says, referring to sister Agathe's *Memories Before and After the Sound of Music*. I protest that I have ordered it, that it is Maria's story I want to hear.

I have come to visit just hours after calling to discuss an old friend's recollections of recorder lessons he took from her at the Trapp Family Lodge decades ago. That was my entrée, but it didn't seem to be working. "There were hundreds of students. I don't

✦ ✦ ✦ ✦ ✦ ✦ ✦ ✦ ✦ ✦ ✦ ✦ ✦ ✦ ✦ ✦ ✦ ✦ ✦ ✦ ✦ ✦ ✦ ✦ ✦ ✦

remember him," says Maria, reading the e-mail exchanges with my friend. "And he says these were *private* lessons. I don't think I ever gave private lessons." Ah, well. Nobody's fault. It's been fifty years. Memories dissipate.

Maria is a vigorous ninety-three, with a white, waist-length pony-tail and still as involved with music as she was more than three-quarters of a century ago. The music stand in the living room of her chalet a mile or so from the lavish grounds of the lodge contains scores for both recorder and accordion. "I can play chords on the accordion, but just the melody on the recorder," she says.

A week after our conversation, Agathe's book arrived. Here is part of what I learned: The Trapp Family Singers, who gave concerts in thirty countries from 1936 to 1956, moved from Austria to the United States in 1938, just before the outbreak of World War II. Their repertoire consisted of sacred music, folk songs, and sixteenth- and seventeenth-century madrigals, sung in English, Italian, and German. Guests who visit the lodge expect Trapp family descendants to break into "Edelweiss" or "Do-Re-Mi" at the drop of an alpenhorn. Few realize that Richard Rodgers and Oscar Hammerstein created this and the other songs for *The Sound of Music* years after the Trapp Family Singers had stopped singing professionally. The distortion of facts structured to accommodate a plot written around these songs brought worldwide acclaim to the family, for reasons that both dis-tressed and bewildered them. For the most part, though, they are reconciled to the fact that both movie and play have contributed greatly to their lasting fame.

This summary—terse but accurate—convinces Maria that I have done my homework, and we speak again.

She talks a bit about her thirty-two years as a lay missionary in Papua, New Guinea. "I taught singing, did medical work . . . what-ever was needed." Sister Rosemarie and brother Johannes (who now runs the lodge) went with her as well. "Johannes stayed for the first two and one-half years and learned the language perfectly.

He built a school, a church, and a house for me. Rosemarie taught down there for four years. When we came home for a break, which I had to do occasionally just to get away from the trop- ics, she stayed home and I returned. She now conducts sing-alongs for guests at the lodge."

Others were no less dedicated. Rupert was a family doctor in Ver- mont. Werner ran a dairy farm in Waitsfield before his retirement some years ago. (Both enlisted in the Tenth Mountain Division as ski troopers in World War II and fought the Germans in Italy.) Agathe founded a kindergarten in Maryland, which she ran for thirty-seven years. Hedwig, whose severe asthma forced her to live in Hawaii's more forgiving climate, taught youngsters there for several years.

Photo courtesy Trapp FamLodge

In a modest chalet near Trapp Lodge, Maria attends family and lodge functions, but mostly pursues her own interests.

When Maria returned from New Guinea in 1988 at age seventy- four, she brought with her a twenty-six-year-old Tanzanian, Kikuli Mwanukuzi, whom she later adopted. Kikuli, a math tutor at Johnson State College, has aspirations of being governor of Vermont one day. I ask if he has his citizenship. "Not yet," he says, "but it won't be long. If Schwarzenegger can do it, why can't I?"

Directions: To reach the Trapp Family Lodge, take Route 100 north to the outskirts of Stowe. Take a left on Moscow Road and follow the signs to 100 Trapp Hill Road. For more information visit www .trappfamily.com, or call (800) 826-7000.

★ ★ ★ ★ ★ ★ ★ ★ ★ ★ ★ ★ ★ ★ ★ ★ ★ ★ ★ ★ ★ ★ ★ ★ ★ ★ ★ ★ ★ ★ ★

## High School Dropout Transforms College Education
Strafford

A goodly number of this country's 105 land grant colleges and universities—Iowa State, Cornell University, the University of Vermont, and Washington State University among them—have a Morrill Hall on campus. Largely this is because if it weren't for Senator Justin Smith Morrill, those institutions would not exist. In 1862 President Abraham Lincoln signed the Morrill Land-Grant Colleges Act, written and fought for by Senator Morrill for the previous seven years. This act allocated funds from the sales of public lands to support new colleges that taught agriculture, engineering, business, and home economics. It opened the door for poor and minority students to pursue a college education.

Justin Morrill grew up in Strafford, Vermont, and eagerly looked forward to attending college, but his family was too poor to send him. He left school for good at age fifteen. His interest in architecture, horticulture, and politics, though, was intense enough for him to become learned in all three. After seventeen years as a merchant and seven as a farmer, Morrill was elected to the Congress, and eventually the U.S. Senate, serving in one body or another for nearly fifty years. Today more than 25 million graduates have Senator Morrill to thank for their college education.

The Gothic Revival homestead and farm complex in Strafford was designed by Justin Morrill and built for him in 1848. The house is furnished with original and family pieces. Interpretive exhibits are located in several of the barns and outbuildings.

Directions: From Route 132 in South Strafford, take the Justin Smith Morrill Highway and go 2 miles to the Strafford Village. The homestead is located on the right-hand side of the road on the north end of the village. The homestead is open from Memorial Day to Columbus Day, Saturday and Sunday 11:00 a.m. to 5:00 p.m. For more information visit www.morrillhomestead.org.

## RIP, Bovinity Divinity

Waterbury

Up an imposing hill and beyond a much less imposing parking lot, a white picket fence surrounds a grove of beech trees. In these peaceful confines you'll find Ben & Jerry's Flavor Graveyard, a repository for ill-named or ill-conceived ice cream concoctions that have failed the test of consumer approval. I was looking for a headstone that commemorated a real doozy, perhaps a Garlic Lamb Fat Fudge Swirl or a Carrot Tomato Vegan Delight. Instead I spy a dead flavor I would have graded a definite keeper: Maine Blueberry Ice Cream. What could have happened? Was it too down home? Too ordinary? No. Too seasonal. From the inscription I learn that when summer faded, this flavor's sales did as well.

But here's an envelope pusher even I could have predicted: Tennessee Mud had Loser stamped on its one-pint carton from at least

Cocoanut Cream Pie Low-Fat Ice Cream, Honey Apple Raisin Chocolate Cookie, KaBerry KABOOM! Lemon Peppermint Carob Chip, Makin' Whoopee Pie, Ooey Gooey Cake Low-Fat Frozen Yogurt, Peanuts! Popcorn!, Peppermint Schtick . . . Had enough?

two directions. Bourbon lovers looking for a taste treat reminding
them of a favored beverage—and perhaps a wee buzz?—turned
up their noses. Parents fearing residual traces of alcohol likely were
driven to the safer scoops of Howard Johnson's 31 Flavors, or a local
ice creamery. (The ingredients were said to include a taste of "Jack
Daniel's Old No. 7 Tennessee Sour Mash Whiskey," a contention the
B&J public relations department, after several phone calls, would neither confirm nor deny.) The epitaph says it all:

> THE BOTTLE IS EMPTY,
> THE CUP AND THE GLASS.
> MUD WITH JACK DANIEL'S
> WAS NOT MEANT TO LAST.
> 1988–1989

Discovering other flavors that deserved capital punishment, you
may be as glad as I was to hear that Economic Crunch, Honey I'm
Home, and Bovinity Divinity have gotten their just desserts.

The Flavor Graveyard is on the grounds of Ben & Jerry's Waterbury factory, the company's flagship manufacturing plant. Ben &
Jerry's happens to be one of the nation's best companies in terms of
social responsibility, their mission reading, in part: "Initiating ways
to improve the quality of life locally, nationally, and internationally."
Even after being absorbed by corporate giant Unilever, B&J has been
able to retain and act on its long-held progressive values.

Directions: Take I-89 exit 10 and go north on Route 100 North.
The factory is up a mile on the left. Tours at the Waterbury factory
are conducted seven days a week year-round, except for Thanksgiv-
ing, Christmas, and New Year's Day. Hours vary by season. For more
information visit www.benjerry.com/scoop_shops/factory_tour or call
(802) 882-1240, extension 2285.

## Spiderweb Man
Williamstown

"I have a grandson, " says Will Knight, "a graduate of Rensselaer. Had a job before he even got out of college. He's a crackerjack on the computer."

"'Gramps,' he says to me one day—he was like fifteen or six-teen—'you oughta get on that Internet.'

"I said, 'You know, you're the second guy to tell me that.'" He pauses for effect. "'I told the first guy *I* was the original Web site.'"

You can almost hear the rim shot. Will's timing and delivery are superb, as if he's told this story a thousand times, which of course he has. "So my grandson says, 'I'll put you right on it, Gramps.' And the next thing you know, I had a Web site."

We're at Knight's Spider Web Farm, said to be the only one of its kind in the world. Forty years ago, Will moved to Vermont from Brooklyn with his wife and four children. A professional real estate appraiser, he got a job with the state transportation department while Interstate 91 was being built, negotiating with families who were displaced by the construction. "We took a lot of houses up there," he says. "Fifty-six in Saint Johnsbury alone."

But when the highway was finished, Will was out of a job. He was a good woodworker, though, and built miniature cabinets to sell at craft shows around the state. But he soon tired of the constant travel, and few people wanted to come to him.

"One day my wife collected a spiderweb on a piece of wood and painted a flower on it," he recalls. "A fellow came in, looked around, and asked if we had any plain webs. He said, 'If you did, I think you'd have a market.'

"Then for some reason, I forget why, I got invited to Faneuil Hall, in Boston—a huge market. I took about 500 webs down there, and in a week we sold about 350. So I came back and built more web frames. See that shed out there? There's space in it for about 300

★ ★ ★ ★ ★ ★ ★ ★ ★ ★ ★ ★ ★ ★ ★ ★ ★ ★ ★ ★ ★ ★ ★ ★ ★ ★ ★ ★

webs. I can get 275 more in the garage, and another 240 in those metal frames next to it."

Will has perfected his business over the years by listening to ideas from friends. And each improvement has its own story.

"One day back then a guy came in, a friend of my wife's from community college and a business planner in the Salmon administration [Vermont governor Tom Salmon, 1973–1977]. Bert was his name. He came in and looked at one of my webs and said, 'What are you going to do with this?'

"I say, 'It hangs on the wall, Bert. It's a plaque. What you think of it?'

"'Pretty,' he says. Then a minute later he says, 'Look around the room and tell me what you see—everything that hangs there.'

"'Bert,' I say, 'no games! Tell me what I can do to improve things.'

"'Well, I'm telling you,' he says. 'Everything hanging in this room has a frame, *except your plaques.*'

"And then I saw it. This was a way to finish my product! And that's the way these things happen."

Will on pricing:

**Will Knight is gonna kill me. First of all, Spider Web Farm is a lovely place up the hill, and *not* the building right across the road. It just seemed like a good picture. Sorry, Will!**

★ ★ ★ ★ ★ ★ ★ ★ ★ ★ ★ ★ ★ ★ ★ ★ ★ ★ ★ ★ ★ ★ ★ ★ ★

"A friend of mine in Barre—big-time kitchen developer—told me I wasn't getting enough money for these plaques. He first told me that thirty years ago when I was getting $4.95.

"'Willy, you're making a mistake. You're giving them away. What the hell is $4.95,' he says. 'You gotta sell twenty to make $100. Why don't you ask $50, and then you'll only have to sell two!'

"I say, 'Claude, who the hell is going to pay $50 for a plaque?'

"'You'll see,' he said. And he was right. A man came in a month later with his wife. I had one hanging up here—a big one—and I had written on it with white correction fluid, as a joke: "Goodby Wilbur." [For those who haven't read *Charlotte's Web*, Wilbur is the pig afraid of ending up on the dinner table.] His wife was looking around outside, and he came over to my counter with the plaque. "I'll take this one," he said.

"I said, 'Sorry, That's not for sale.'

"'I don't think you heard me,' he said. 'I'll take it.'

"So I walked around the counter and got a big bag; I put the plaque in the bag with one of my flyers and said: 'Now is that going to be cash or credit?'

"He says, 'Cash.' He never asked me how much it was.

So I said, 'Okay, that'll be one hundred plus tax. He never said a word!

"He says to his wife, 'Agnes,' he says, 'I got one for your class.' It turns out she's a teacher and he's a superintendent of schools from wherever the hell they came from, and she does a whole unit on *Charlotte's Web*. I felt bad. For a hundred bucks. But not *my* hundred bucks! Well, it is now."

Directions: How Will Knight gets those spiderwebs on his plaques is another good story—as well as how Spider Web Farm got its name. To hear a few of Will's stories and check out his web plaques, take exit 5 on I-89 toward Williamstown, and stay on Route 14 going south through the village. Turn right onto Spider Web Farm Road, the naming of which is another good story. For more information visit www.spiderwebfarm.com or call (802) 433-5568.

# 7

## Lower Champlain Valley

**A good chunk** of the Lake Champlain Maritime Museum's exhibits are hidden—some 350 feet or more beneath the lake's surface. So how do interested parties see them? Until 2004 only certified scuba divers had access. That was the year that museum technicians discovered a way to equip their remotely operated vehicles (ROVs) with video equipment that could project live underwater pictures directly to visitors in tour boats. What treasures await!

Once in a while a personal story comes along that just feels good to tell. For more than fifteen years, Pat Palmer of Bristol has conducted one of the most unique and self-contained trash collection systems ever devised. His two associates, Spud and Chief, are full-fledged partners, and the entire operation would go to seed without them. What a team!

Decades before the Civil War, an "underground railroad" of men and women helped runaway slaves who had escaped their lives of desperation but had nowhere to go. Some "agents" for the fugitives hid them temporarily until a family up north was found to offer employment and education. The Robinsons, in Ferrisburgh, were such a family. The Rokeby Museum tells their story, and those of the dozens of men and women who lived with them until they were prepared for new lives of freedom in Vermont or elsewhere.

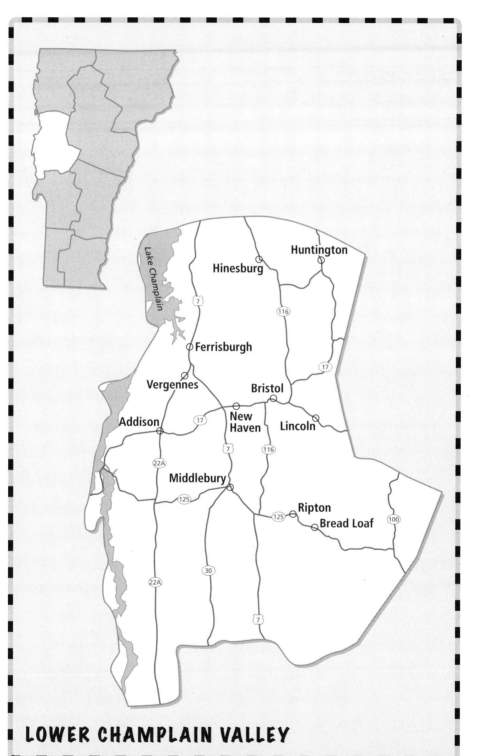

Lake Champlain

Huntington

Hinesburg

7

116

Ferrisburgh

17

Vergennes

Bristol

Addison

17

New Haven

Lincoln

22A

7

116

Middlebury

125

Ripton

125

Bread Loaf

100

22A

30

7

LOWER CHAMPLAIN VALLEY

# Vermont's Sheep Heyday

In Vermont's sheep heyday Addison County counted 373 sheep per square mile. This Vermont County raised more sheep and produced more wool, in proportion to its size and population, than any other county in the United States. The Vermont sheep industry allowed a burgeoning wool-processing industry to arise here as well. Carding mills, which first appeared in Vermont in the 1790s, combed raw wool to prepare it for spinning. Fulling mills washed and sized the woof fiber, or woolen cloth. In 1829 Vermont had twenty-nine carding mills and fifty-eight fulling mills. By 1820 there were four times as many of these mills throughout the state.

## Vermont's One-of-a-Kind Garbage Pick-up Service

Bristol

For thirty years, Bristol's road crew had picked up the town's garbage every week. But when a new administrator came to town, he decided the road crew should *remain* on the road, and that garbage pick up should be privatized. Patrick Palmer's bid was the lowest, so he was awarded the contract. Pat didn't have a truck, but he did have a wagon and a team of horses. He lived in New Haven just one town away and figured that a job covering roughly 300 homes and businesses seemed manageable. And it was, for the next nine years. Then two years ago a Bristol official said the town could not afford Pat anymore.

"They wouldn't give me a deal to dump the trash in their landfill, which is still open," says Pat. So he got in touch with Scott Olson, a division manager for Casella Waste Systems, which services the Middlebury area. "I asked him if Casella wanted to buy my business. Instead he asked me what *I* wanted to do. I said I liked the job and wanted to keep doing it."

Upshot: Pat and Scott Olson worked out an arrangement whereby every Friday instead of going to the Bristol landfill, Pat transfers both trash and recycled materials onto one of Casella's rear loaders at a drop-off point in town. Not only does Casella charge Pat half as much per bag as he paid the town; the company accepts the recycling preseparated, as opposed to Pat separating paper from bottles from cans, and so on, himself.

So this becomes an illustration not only of Vermont ingenuity at its best, but a rare example of a corporation serving both community and entrepreneur, at the expense of primacy to the bottom line. "We're a part of the community," says Olson, who now runs a division of Casella in Geneva, New York. "We try to determine what a community's needs are, and service them any way we can. This was an opportunity to do just that."

Even Pat Palmer needs a day off once in a while. Here a few friends help out on Pat's Bristol rounds. Question: When do Chief and Spud get *their* day off?

★ ★ ★ ★ ★ ★ ★ ★ ★ ★ ★ ★ ★ ★ ★ ★ ★ ★ ★ ★ ★ ★ ★ ★ ★ ★ ★ ★ ★

To continue in a parallel vein, here is how Pat has arranged his
business (keep in mind he has no tractors, only horses): On his farm
he raises hay, with the help of his horses, Chief and Spud, for all
planting, cultivating, and harvesting. He feeds the hay to his horses,
which not only eat well but supply the manure (and the horsepower
to spread it), to in turn help ensure a good crop. The horses' good
health allows them to work with Pat to collect the community's trash
and recyclables over time, which in turn helps to complete another
cycle—that of man's attempt to better live in harmony with nature,
which indeed is what this particular man is doing.

Now to the intrigue that, if one looks for it, is part of just about
any vocation. Pat has his customers buy yellow stickers at Martin's
Hardware that they put on each bag for collection. (The recycling is
free.) Sometimes a crafty customer will "forget" to put on a sticker.
Sometimes a less-than-honest customer will steal a sticker from
another bag. Sometimes a customer will wrap half a sticker around
the plastic string at the top of some bags, on the grounds that it
will be appear to be a whole sticker. Pat, ever vigilant, knows all the
tricks. Those unstickered or semistickered bags remain uncollected,
until the misdemeanors are rectified.

Not that Pat or his horses are off-duty every day but Friday. There
is sap to be collected in the spring, sleigh rides in the winter, carriage
rides for weddings, wagon rides for special events, and wood to be
gathered. "I also do some logging for people and occasionally pull a
moose out of the national forest in season." He's had the team he
uses now for seven years. As a general rule they have a working life
of up to fifteen years.

So do the horses get any leisure time?

"Oh yeah," says Pat. "Just as much as I do."

If you're in Bristol on a Friday—or any other day Pat happens to be
out and about—make it a point to wave to him. You could say hi to
Chief and Spud, too. Better yet, ask Pat if it's okay to give them a carrot.

## The Great Bristol Outhouse Race

Bristol

Let's say you're in Bristol next Fourth of July and want to take part in the festivities. One possibility is the traditional Outhouse Race, run just before the parade, in which competing outhouse contestants race one another to a finish line. The outhouses are on wheels, and the teams consist of one member sitting on the seat and two runners outside it, either pushing or pulling their vehicle of necessity. (Outhouse decoration rules require a door—"for privacy, of course.") Members of the crowd can bet on their favorite entrant in a heat by buying tickets of the color assigned to that entrant and for that heat. All tickets are numbered and double, so the purchaser gets one half and the seller retains the other half..

An annual Bristol ritual before the Fourth of July parade is the Outhouse Race, fiercely fought contests among the three-person teams—two running outside and one on the seat.

Betting on your favorite entrant, though, takes a bit of concentration. Following is the first part of a description of a "Sample Race," as prepared by the officials:

★ ★ ★ ★ ★ ★ ★ ★ ★ ★ ★ ★ ★ ★ ★ ★ ★ ★ ★ ★ ★ ★ ★ ★ ★ ★

"Suppose in the first heat that the entrants are teams W, X, Y, and Z. Team W has been assigned the red ticket color, team X has been assigned the blue ticket color, team Y has been assigned the orange ticket color, and team Z has been assigned the yellow ticket color. You wish to bet that team X will win this heat. You then buy a blue ticket from a seller, who is a member of the Bristol Rotary Club and is wearing a sandwich board listing the names of the entrants for this first heat and the ticket color assigned to each. This information is also posted at the registration desk and announced over the public address system. There is generally no shortage of ticket sellers. The first heat is run, and team Y is declared the winner. Team Y was assigned the orange color, which means that your blue ticket can be properly discarded, along with all the other blue tickets, red tickets and yellow tickets sold for the first heat."

The hypothetical results of subsequent heats are just as thoroughly described. Fortunately, a fifteen- to twenty-minute interlude between heats will give wagering spectators a chance to clear their heads. Our advice: If you'd like either to run the race or bet on it, read the rules, race explanation, and sample race description online well before you arrive. See www.midvermont.com/area_info/bristol_outhouse_race.shtml.

### A Museum of Treasures, Both Seen and Unseen
Ferrisburgh

You might think that those visitors to the Lake Champlain Maritime Museum interested in underwater exhibits but without scuba certification (roughly 98 percent of the U.S. population) would miss out completely. Not so. Beginning in 2004, the utilization of remotely operated underwater vehicles (ROVs) now allows everyone an opportunity to see the shipwrecks. The museum has been using ROVs since the 1980s, some having been sent down to sites of more than 350 feet. Staffers ultimately realized that this tool was also a way to more fully share the extraordinary underwater resources with the public.

The twelve-bolt helmet was used by deep-sea divers from the 1830s to the 1970s, until it was replaced by SCUBA equipment. Try one on at the Lake Champlain Maritime Museum!

Executive director and cofounder Art Cohn is quick to define the museum's mission as one "preserving and sharing the history and archaeology of the region, and the study and management of underwater cultural resources." According to Cohn, the exhibit that most thoroughly embodies this mission, as well as the museum's ongoing work, is the one featuring the canal schooner *General Butler.*

"It's a perfect example of underwater resource management," says Cohn. "The 88-foot wooden remains of a canal boat located in Burlington harbor . . . has been a major focus of our research. True heroism was involved in the rescue of the shipwrecked people. It has the blue-collar, day-to-day commerce these boats represented. It has the canal era, a major focus of our study. And it's got underwater

resource management all over it." A full-sized replica displayed in the museum is modeled from detailed archaeological measurements.

Sunk in a violent storm in December 1876, the *General Butler* was discovered by divers in 1980. Here is its story, taken from contemporary eyewitness and press accounts: William Montgomery was captaining the *General Butler* (named after a Massachusetts lawyer and Civil War hero) one Saturday in December when heavy gales drove the vessel toward the Burlington breakwater. *General Butler* was carrying a load of Isle La Motte marble for delivery to the Burlington Marble Works. Also on board were a deckhand, Montgomery's teenage daughter Cora and her schoolgirl friend, and a quarry operator from Isle La Motte.

The power of the storm was too much for the steering mechanism of the aging schooner, and just off the breakwater, the vessel began to drift southward. The deckhand threw over the storm anchor in a vain attempt to keep the vessel from crashing into the breakwater's stone-filled cribs. Meanwhile, Captain Montgomery chained a spare tiller bar onto the ship's steering gear. He then ordered the anchor line severed with an axe and attempted to round the southern end of the breakwater, but despite his efforts, a short distance from the southern lighthouse, *General Butler* instead smashed into the breakwater.

The passengers and crew were able to leap free of the wreckage onto the breakwater. The captain was last to leave the ship and barely made it to safety after jumping at the crest of a large wave. The *General Butler* sank immediately, its stone cargo propelling it downward. Stranded on the open breakwater, whipped by fierce winds and driving snow, the canal boat's refugees might have died were it not for James Wakefield and his son, Jack. The two untied a small government lighthouse boat and rowed out to the breakwater. Captain Montgomery lifted his daughter and her friend into James Wakefield's arms and then clambered aboard himself after the deckhand and the quarry operator had jumped into the bobbing rowboat.

Although the masts, rigging, and some other equipment were recovered, the hull of the *General Butler* was not. Today, it rests in 40 feet of water at the south end of Burlington's breakwater. You'll be able to imagine for yourself what it was like aboard an 1862-class canal boat by climbing the gangplank of the schooner *Lois McClure*, in residence at the museum's Basin Harbor facility during the summer and used as a periodic teaching tool in Vermont and New York schools and communities.

Another era of underwater resource management goes back a century earlier, to the Revolutionary War. During the Battle of Valcour Bay on Lake Champlain in 1776, General Benedict Arnold led a naval force against the British, the colonists with half the ships and firepower. Although Arnold lost what is considered the first battle fought by the U.S. Navy, he delayed the British forces by a full year, which led to their defeat at Saratoga in 1777. During the course of Arnold's nighttime retreat after a day of devastating losses on both sides, the British caught up to his diminished fleet near Crown Point, on the New York side of the lake. Arnold's Ship made it to shore, where it was set afire before the crew escaped.

The museum's Valcour Bay Research Project involves systematically mapping the submerged battlefield left behind at Valcour Island. So far, several hundred artifacts have been mapped in place while a small selection of exhibit-quality artifacts have been recovered. The *Philadelphia II* is an exact, full-size reproduction of one of Benedict Arnold's gunboats. The original *Philadelphia* was located and recovered in 1935. It is currently on display at the Smithsonian Institution. An important related project under way is a management plan for the *Spitfire*, the last unaccounted-for gunboat from Benedict Arnold's fleet.

This is a simple sample of the surprises that await a curious visitor to the Lake Champlain Maritime Museum. Spend some time on its Web site to familiarize yourself with the range of available activities and outreach programs (kindergarten through graduate school), and the opportunity to observe boat-building and blacksmithing in working shops.

★ ★ ★ ★ ★ ★ ★ ★ ★ ★ ★ ★ ★ ★ ★ ★ ★ ★ ★ ★ ★ ★ ★ ★ ★ ★ ★ ★ ★

Directions: Follow U.S. Route 4 to Route 22A, and drive north 40 miles to Vergennes. Turn left on Panton Road, and go 1 mile. Then turn right on Basin Harbor Road, and go 6 miles to the museum on right, at 4472 Basin Harbor Road. The museum is open late May through late October, 10:00 a.m. to 5:00 p.m. daily. To get an idea of the host of activities the maritime museum provides, inquire about visiting the *Lois McClure,* or find out general information, visit www. lcmm.org, or call (802) 475-2022.

## Vermont's Underground Railroad

Ferrisburgh

On a ninety-acre site on U.S. Route 7 in Ferrisburgh is the Rokeby Museum, a National Historic Landmark judged to be the best documented stop on the Underground Railway. In the decades leading up to the Civil War, Rowland T. Robinson and his wife, Rachel, harbored dozens of fugitive slaves at their farm and provided them with the employment and education that would prepare them to start new lives in the North.

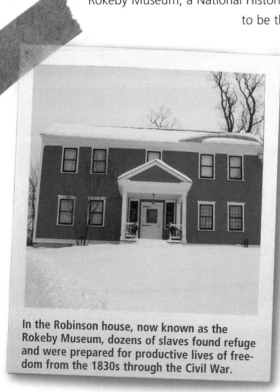

In the Robinson house, now known as the Rokeby Museum, dozens of slaves found refuge and were prepared for productive lives of freedom from the 1830s through the Civil War.

The Robinsons were devout Quakers who believed that slavery was a sin to be opposed by every acceptable means. The thousands of letters in the family's collection reveal exactly what the escaped slaves went through as they risked severe punishment or worse to escape their lives of desperation. Some of these letters offer illuminating case studies of specific individuals, lending identities to their customary anonymity.

What one takes from an experience at Rokeby Museum is the realization that for those fugitive slaves who made it as far as Vermont, there would be no more hiding for fear of capture. Somewhat farther south—in a slave border state like Maryland, for example, or a free border state like Pennsylvania—runaway slaves were generally caught. They had to travel with utmost caution until they reached Massachusetts, at least. Sometimes antislavery agents in states south of Vermont performed a service similar to that of recruiters and personnel counselors today, attempting to match a prospective employee's skills and accomplishments with an employer's perceived needs. The following letter excerpts, for example, were compiled by Rokeby Museum director Jane Williamson as part of a winter 2001 *Vermont History* article.

One correspondent was Oliver Johnson, a Vermonter and newspaper editor who helped a number of fugitives from states to the south. In 1837 Johnson wrote Rowland Robinson from Jenner Township in Pennsylvania. The runaway he had found, Simon, was wanted for a sizable reward.

"When he came here, he was destitute of clothing, and unable to proceed," wrote Johnson. "William C. Griffith, the son of a friend, who has often rendered assistance to runaways, kindly offered to keep him until spring. . . . It is not considered safe for him to remain here after winter has gone by, as search will no doubt be made for him.

"He is 28 years old," Johnson continued, "and appeared to me to be an honest, likely man. . . . I was so well pleased with his appearance that I could not help thinking he would be a good man for you to hire. Mr. Griffith says that he is very trustworthy, of a kind disposition, and

knows how to do almost all kinds of farm work. He is used to teaming, and is very good to manage horses. He says that he could beat any man in the neighborhood where he lived at mowing, cradling, or pitching."

New York City Quaker and store owner Joseph Beale said of fugitive Jeremiah Snowden in 1842 that "Brother John Nickolson thinks Jeremiah can be very useful to a farmer needing such a man." And later that it would be "safer for him to be in Massachusetts or Vermont if work is to be had for him. We were unwilling to risk his remaining, although we had abundance of work for him at this busy season."

New York Quaker and antislavery agent Charles Marriott assured Robinson that John Williams "was a good chopper and farmer," and that his wife, Martha, was "useful and well conducted in the house. . . . The recent decision of the Supreme Court as to the unconstitutionality of jury trial laws for them has decided us to send them further north either to you or to Canada. . . . If they could be taken in by thee, we should think them safer."

Each of the correspondents makes clear to the fugitives that Vermont is a safe haven, and that those few who had considered going as far as Canada had no need to do so. In its day Rokeby was one of the most prosperous farms in the Champlain Valley, and an ideal transitional destination for slaves preparing themselves for lives as free men and women.

On-site are the main house and most of the original outbuildings, plus hiking trails over more than fifty acres of farmland and orchards. The house may be seen by guided tour in groups limited to twelve. Tours last forty-five minutes.

Directions: On U.S. Route 7, 2 miles south of the North Ferrisburgh village center, watch for the historic site marker and front entrance sign on the east side of the road. The museum is open from mid-May to mid-October. House tours are offered three times a day, Thursday through Sunday, but the rest of the farm and museum are open to self-guided tours. For more information visit www.rokeby.org or call (802) 877-3406.

## The Crash on Camel's Hump

Huntington

A little before 2:00 a.m. on October 16, 1947, a U.S. Army Air Corps B-24 was on a training mission from Westover Field in Chicopee, Massachusetts, to give copilot John Ramasocky practice in instrument flying. To prevent his visual contact with the ground, a canvas hood surrounded his side of the cockpit.

Lieutenant David Potter, the pilot, checked the plane's altitude visually, and Ramasocky studied his instruments. It was a clear night, but there was no moon and the plane was over sparsely populated hills with 6 inches of new snow. This combination of factors, historian Brian Lindner believes, significantly reduced the pilot's depth perception. The lights of Burlington appeared, and the plane turned right toward Manchester, New Hampshire. Five minutes later it slammed into Camel's Hump, which at 4,083 feet is Vermont's third-highest peak.

Like many crashes this one could have been avoided by the presence of an individual qualified to make a lifesaving decision—had fate not kept him off the flight. Just before the B-24 left Westover Field, a flight instructor assigned to observe the crew's performance was ordered to return to the hangar area. Ten men died in the 1947 B-24 crash. Top gunner and private first class James Wilson was the only survivor. A rescue party reached him at dusk, two days after the crash. Wilson had suffered a bad head gash and a broken knee. Even worse, he was exposed to 20-degree weather during those two days, as well as during the rescue party's arduous descent from Camel's Hump the following day. This left him with frostbite that required the amputation, as Brian Lindner writes, "of most of both arms and legs." Four years after the crash, James Wilson returned to Vermont to thank his Civilian Air Patrol rescuers personally. He then went on to a successful career as a lawyer, retiring to Florida in 1989. He died in 2000.

Directions: Camel's Hump State Park is the largest state park in Vermont. To access it from the west, take I-89 exit 11. Go east on

★ ★ ★ ★ ★ ★ ★ ★ ★ ★ ★ ★ ★ ★ ★ ★ ★ ★ ★ ★ ★ ★ ★ ★ ★ ★

Route 2 to Richmond Village and take a right onto Bridge Street, crossing the Winooski River to Richmond's historic Old Round Church. Bear right at the church onto the Richmond-Huntington Road and follow it approximately 8 miles to Huntington Center. Turn left on Camel's Hump Road, and follow it 3.5 miles to the trailhead. For more information and a map of the park, see www.central-vt .com/visit/attract/camhump.

## A Good $2 Mechanic Is Hard to Find

Lincoln

Actually, it turns out—at least around here—a good $2 mechanic is impossible to find. Some time ago I read an essay by correspondent Chris Bohjalian on the Hallmark Channel's New Morning show about Nick Norton, a Lincoln resident and part-time mechanic (he's only eleven, so school and his chores come first). Storyline: Nick was so good he was not only able to charge $2 an hour; he had a stable of regular customers.

I called on a snowy Sunday in December to see how this veteran— he started his business when he was eight—had evolved. We talked first about the way Nick's winter work differs from the jobs he lines up for the spring. "I work on snowmobiles and plow driveways, mostly," he said. "For the bigger jobs I have a snowplow that goes on the front of my tractor. For smaller jobs I put a snow bucket on my lawn mower. The longest driveway is probably my grandma's. That's about 450 feet."

Then we got down to some nitty-gritty. Was Nick still charging $2 an hour? No, he was up to $3 and $4 an hour these days. He charges $3 an hour for haying, and $4 for engine repair work. "I realized that it takes more time, because I fix more of the extreme stuff now. I don't just sharpen blades and change oil and batteries. I can fix a broken mower deck, too."

I mentioned that about the time Chris Bohjalian talked with him, he had just bought some hydraulic hoses for a front loader he was going to build for his John Deere 140. "Yep, the front loader is finished. I bought snow tires, too, so I can use it for my bigger snow-plowing jobs." See that? Nick isn't the least bit reluctant to plow his profits back into capital investment, a classic strategy for maximizing small-business growth.

Nick Norton has run his own business since he was eight. Somehow he balances school, chores, and repair work, with time to play.

After the snow is gone, though, there's mud month to get through. That's when the action starts down at his dad's sugarhouse. Nick will do whatever is needed, whether it's tapping, boiling, or packaging.

When that's over, it will be time to think about what new entrepreneurial challenges await him next spring. "I like what I do," says Nick. "If I've learned anything, it's probably that I want to be a mechanic when I grow up." A mechanic with a sizable head start over his competition, for sure.

### Robert Frost—The Bread Loaf Years

Ripton

Robert Frost spent his Vermont years either in Shaftsbury, in the south, or in Ripton, in the central part of the state. It was in Ripton that Frost developed a forty-year attachment to the prestigious Bread Loaf Writers' Conference, which he founded in 1926.

★ ★ ★ ★ ★ ★ ★ ★ ★ ★ ★ ★ ★ ★ ★ ★ ★ ★ ★ ★ ★ ★ ★ ★ ★ ★ ★

Frost bought the Noble farm in 1938 and lived there summers until 1963. Late In 2007 the farmhouse was vandalized, to the shock of neighbors and distant Frost-lovers alike.

In 1921 Frost joined the Bread Loaf School of English, started the year before at Middlebury College. The Bread Loaf Mountain campus, vacant from mid-August to the end of the month, struck Frost as an ideal location to convene writers eager to improve their skills, with the help of established professionals who would serve as mentors. He made this idea stick and in 1926 presided over the Bread Loaf Writers' Conference inaugural session.

Until 1962, the year before he died, Frost was there nearly every year, as faculty member, speaker, or fellow. He was so ubiquitous, in fact, that writer and editor Louis Untermeyer referred to Bread Loaf as "the most Frost-bitten place in America." Frost himself had mixed feelings about the direction of the conference, in particular a growing emphasis on matching writers with editors and literary agents. He once called Bread Loaf the Two Weeks' Manuscript Sales Fair.

After the death of his wife in 1938, Frost bought the Homer Noble Farm in Ripton, comprising several hundred acres of fields and forest near the Bread Loaf campus, including a barn and a cabin. He was so smitten with Kathleen Morrison, a staff member at Bread Loaf and the wife of conference director Ted Morrison, that he asked her to marry him later that same year. She refused but became his secretary for the rest of his life, living in the farmhouse with Ted while Frost occupied the cabin. (No information so far as to what that chain of events did to their respective relationships.) Frost lived there summers until he died in 1963.

Two miles east of Ripton is the Robert Frost Wayside Area, where the Robert Frost Interpretive Trail begins. This idyllic, 3/4-mile tribute to the poet includes seven of his poems mounted on plaques, at intervals on sets dressed by a rushing brook visible beyond the trees or a clearing exposing a Green Mountains backdrop.

Directions: The Robert Frost Memorial Drive, a 14-mile route through woods, farmlands, and mountains, starts at the junction of U.S. Route 7 and Route 125, and 2 miles east of Ripton, on Route 125, is the Robert Frost Wayside Area, where the Robert Frost Interpretive Trail begins. For more information about the Bread Loaf Writers' Conference, visit www.middlebury.edu/academics/blwc.

## When Superlatives Clash

Vergennes

Vergennes lays claim to at least two significant superlatives, each printed on one of the welcome signs at the outskirts of the city. Entering from the west, Vergennes is "the smallest city in Vermont." Entering from the east, it is "the oldest city in Vermont."

Depending on the context, both statements hold water. Because there are only nine cities in the state, by Vermont's technical definition of a city, Vergennes's status as oldest is easy to establish. It bests the charter date of the next oldest city by seventy-seven years. The "smallest city" ranking, though, is more of a problem, primarily because

★ ★ ★ ★ ★ ★ ★ ★ ★ ★ ★ ★ ★ ★ ★ ★ ★ ★ ★ ★ ★ ★ ★ ★ ★ ★ ★ ★ ★ ★

nearly every one of those scrambling for the title has thought of ways to skew the definition to better press its case.

In terms of population alone, Vergennes is a lock. Fifteen hundred fewer people live there than in Newport. In terms of actual square footage, things get murky. Saint Albans appears to have the edge over Vergennes, 2.0 square miles to 2.5. Winooski is even smaller at 1.5 square miles. Winooski has been aggressive in challenging Vergennes for the "smallest" title.

I take this information to Mel Hawley, Vergennes's zoning administrator and former city manager. Mel acknowledges that Winooski had the edge in square miles, but only because Vergennes had resurveyed its boundaries and was therefore honest enough to admit that it was larger than its original charter stipulated.

Bragging rights are a big deal in Vermont. One is for "smallest city."

"If you read our charter," says Mel, "Vergennes is 400 rods by 480 rods. Doing the math, that's a mile and a quarter by a mile and a half. Multiplying 1.25 by 1.5 you get 1.875 square miles. If you look at our tax maps, though, which we did a few years ago, we're taxing on the basis of 1,600 acres. When you do the conversion, Vergennes is 2.5 square miles.

So Vergennes has capitulated to Winooski? "I didn't say that," Mel replies. "Winooski has 6,600 people. That makes us the smallest city in Vermont *by far.*"

Directions: Vergennes is located on Route 22A, 25 miles south of Burlington. For more information visit www.vergennes.org.

# 8

# Northeast Kingdom

**The folks at** *Saint Johnsbury's Fairbanks Museum will roll their eyes when visitors focus on the upper-floor "bug art." There's much else to entrance the most jaded visitor, after all: a planetarium; a meteorological center, with a dozen or more weather forecasts beamed over Vermont Public Radio daily; and 75,000 mounted reptiles, mammals, fish, and birds, including 131 species of hummingbirds, the largest such collection in North America, we're told. But there's no more curiosity-friendly exhibit than the nine works of dead butterflies and beetles arranged to depict historical events. Yes, 13,555 of these poor devils gave their lives to create a display of Old Glory honoring the Articles of Confederation. We're told that the daughter of artist (in quotes?) John Hampson called museums all over the country to plead for bug-art perpetuity before the Fairbanks agreed. There's a relief.*

*Chief Lone Cloud, who heads the Clan of the Hawk of Western Abenaki, is serious about community service. He and a number of Abenaki volunteers present free educational programs throughout the year. On the other hand, he takes himself much less seriously. Under the nom de plume Ralph Swett, the chief writes a weekly column for the* Newport Daily Express *discussing Abenaki as well as local matters, often with a tongue-in-cheek sense of humor. Once he floated the notion that Alexander Twilight, thought to be the first African American college graduate, might actually be Abenaki. "They said he was dark-complected, but he never referred to himself as Black," wrote Ralph. He was only kidding, but not everybody got the joke.*

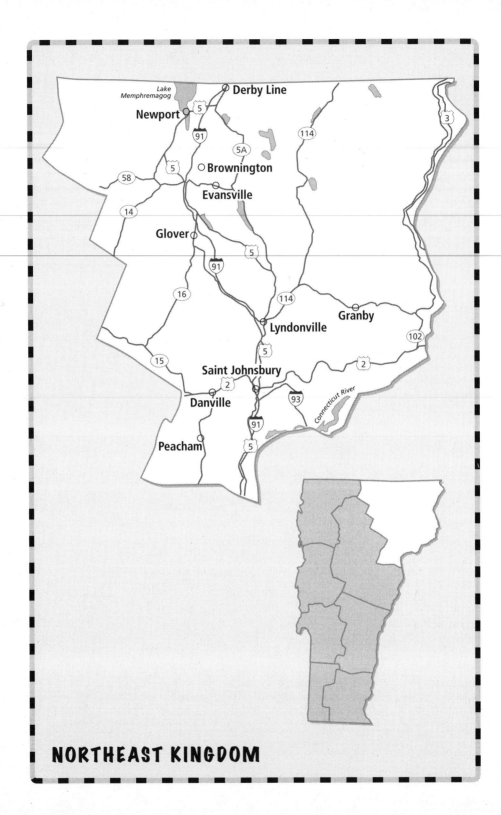

NORTHEAST KINGDOM

## Chief Lone Cloud, Clan of the Hawk of the Western Abenaki Nation

Brownington

Unlike most Native Americans, Vermont's Abenaki were assimilated over the years, not annihilated. (This is not to say that they didn't experience their own share of massacres, as you'll see later in this chapter.) For this peculiar reason the Abenaki have not been federally recognized as a tribe, with all the benefits attending such status. In 2006, though, after decades of wrangling, a bill recognizing the Abenaki Nation as a People was signed by Vermont's governor. This means they are eligible to apply for various federal benefits, and that Abenaki craftsmen can more easily market their products as "Native made." State recognition only, though, also prohibits casinos and grounds for land claims.

This doesn't bother Chief (Ralph Swett) Lone Cloud. "We don't need the BIA [Bureau of Indian Affairs] people around here telling us what to do," he says. Chief Lone Cloud, from Brownington, heads the second-largest Abenaki group in Vermont (the largest being in Swanton, near Lake Champlain). "According to the last census there are 1,700 Abenaki in Vermont," says Ralph. "But I'd say the actual population is probably double that. You understand there are no full-blooded Abenaki here anymore. Everybody is 'part.' We ask those who join us to document their heritage. Those who can't, we accept as associate members. It takes a lot of work to trace the genealogy."

So how does he organize the clan so all the work gets done?

"It's hard. We have a moving population. They come and they go. There are committees, but it's probably the hardest thing I've done in my life—hold a group together. Clearly! A lot of big egos. The old saying 'all chiefs and no Indians,' there's a lot of truth in that, you know?"

The Clan of the Hawk's primary objective is community service. They present free educational programs at schools, libraries, museums, work camps, and prisons throughout the year, concentrating on cultural and societal aspects of the Abenaki tribe, such as its impact on the state of Vermont, its connections to Canada, and various skills and crafts practiced by its people.

The annual Clan of the Hawk Powwow, highlighting Abenaki crafts, rituals, and Native teachings, has been held for seventeen consecutive years.

Much of the clan's funding comes from the Evansville Trading Post, 3 miles down the road. But in a gift-shop warehouse on the powwow grounds next door to his home, Ralph shows me a few craft items. "We formed a craft cooperative quite a few years ago. We're trying to promote people into doing things, rather than sit around feeling sorry for themselves. Here's a history book I wrote in 1975. Here's a coloring book. Here's a picture dictionary translating English into Abenaki. Most everything is made by members of the tribe."

For the first time I notice a title on the chief's shirt, which reads "Chief Spirit Water," and ask how he became Chief Lone Cloud. "We have a benefactor, Chief Looking Glass, from Attleboro, Massachusetts," he says. "He's been one of our elders for many years, and in 2005 he donated more than 1,800 arrowheads, axes, spears,

**Announcing Clan of the Hawk's first cook book! Game recipes from moose and deer to raccoon and skunk; Truly Brave-of-Heart Yellow Jacket soup. $7.99—get yours now!**

stones, and other artifacts to our clan, [and] also birth and death records from eastern Canada and the U.S. going back to the 1600s. We're transcribing them to disk now, so that people can come and listen to them without handling the fragile books.

"Anyway, Chief Looking Glass didn't like the name 'Spirit Water.' He thought the people who named me weren't aware of its derogatory implication. I hadn't thought about it, but when he asked if he could change it to Lone Cloud, I said, 'Sure.'"

For the past eight months or so, Ralph has been writing a weekly column for the *Newport Daily Express*. "We don't muzzle him at all," says *Express* publisher Ken Wells. "We just let him fly." Ralph discusses concerns of not only the Abenaki but also the local populace, often with a tongue-in-cheek sense of humor enjoyed by many but occasionally misunderstood by a few. In a recent column, for example, he proposed that Alexander Twilight, considered the first African American college graduate (and later a minister in Brownington), might actually be Abenaki. "All the old-timers never thought of him being black. They said he was dark complected, but he never referred to himself as black." Shrugging away the controversy, the chief says, "Anyway, I was just having fun, which most people realized."

Last year chemotherapy and radiation treatments for prostate cancer cut into Chief Lone Cloud's school visitation schedule. His last blood test, though, showed that he was cancer free. "Of course they told me that five years ago, too." He also has diabetes, but none of this has slowed him down. "When I got home from the last chemo treatment last spring, I made up my mind I was not going to just sit around and do nothing. Screw it. I'm going to work and just go as hard as I can go. And that's what I've done. The hell with it. If I die, I die."

Directions: To reach the Evansville Trading Post, take exit 26 on Interstate 91, and go east on Route 58 for approximately 6 miles to 645 Evansville Road, Brownington. For information on the annual August powwow and all things Abenaki, see http://clanofthehawkinc .org/default.aspx, or call (802) 754-2817.

★ ★ ★ ★ ★ ★ ★ ★ ★ ★ ★ ★ ★ ★ ★ ★ ★ ★ ★ ★ ★ ★ ★ ★ ★ ★ ★ ★ ★ ★ ★ ★ ★

### Danny Gore—*Easily* Could Have Been the People's Choice
Danville

For thirty-two years Danny Gore represented the unrepresentable—
the imaginary inhabitants of Avery's Gore, in Vermont's Northeast
Kingdom. Danny ran unsuccessfully for governor seventeen consecutive times, beginning in 1962. (Vermont is one of only two states
to elect a governor every two years, rather than four.) When ballots
were being totaled, Danny's were inevitably labeled as "scattered."

Then, in 1994, he took the advice of Senator George Aiken, who
not only named the region where Danny was born and raised but
famously appealed to his U.S. Senate colleagues regarding the Vietnam War: "When in a hopeless campaign, declare victory and go
home." So at noon on Tuesday, November 8, 1994, Danny stood on
the steps of the State House in Montpelier and declared victory. He
officially served as governor for seven minutes, resigned, and went
home to Avery's Gore. (Governor Howard Dean did not acknowledge
this interruption in his power.)

A little context: Back in 1791, the year Vermont became a state,
Westminster sheriff and large landholder Sam Avery lost property
bought years earlier when New York owned it. But the Vermont legislature had already sold much of the good land to speculators, and
Sam got stuck with acreage including what is now called "Avery's
Gore." Gores are triangular or odd-shaped parcels of unincorporated
land, usually rocky or otherwise worthless. They are not part of any
town and are often uninhabited.

"I didn't start out as Danny Gore," says Norm Lewis, a retired educator and the alter ego of Danny Gore. Spanning the entire state and
thirty years, Norm's accomplishments include being a teacher, coach,
principal, and superintendent of schools in, respectively, Cavendish,
Chester, Springfield, Windsor County, and Derby.

Norm reminisces a bit over a delicious lunch at his rambling home in
Danville. The entire Lewis property is one vast museum. Knowing Norm's
weakness for collectibles, friends and acquaintances have filled his base-

ment, garage, and ample barn floor to ceiling with artifacts, eighteenth- and nineteenth-century tools, a steam shed with boiler, a completely outfitted blacksmith shop, vehicles (a 1936 Buick and a 1934 Diamond T dump truck), and a 20-foot-high working railroad semaphore, from Norm's eighteen years as an engineer on the Mount Washington cog railway.

Photo courtesy of the author

Representing the downtrodden, the underrepresented, and the nonexistent, Danny Gore has worked tirelessly for his constituency—running unsuccessfully for governor seventeen times.

Lunch, by the way, is completely homemade, from the excellent pea soup, the two kinds of sandwiches (ham salad and egg salad on bread baked by Norm), to a raspberry shortcake for dessert. "My wife died in 2000, but I often helped with the cooking," he says.

"I was doing political humor on the side," Norm says of Danny Gore's origin, "and enrolled in a theater class. I hated to write out my own material, so I made a tape and gave it to a student in my class whose dad made records in Springfield. When I picked up the record, 'Rep. Danny Gore' was on the label. At the time I was known

★ ★ ★ ★ ★ ★ ★ ★ ★ ★ ★ ★ ★ ★ ★ ★ ★ ★ ★ ★ ★ ★ ★ ★ ★ ★ ★ ★ ★

as Representative Lewis, from the town of Lewis. Where Danny Gore came from, I have no idea. So I just moved my political base to Avery's Gore, where nobody has ever lived.

"I still do some gigs, just not as many as I used to. For example, I was just down to Tunbridge Fair. I've never had an agent, and I don't advertise; but I do get calls. I got a call once from the Woodstock Inn. They were hosting businessmen from England, who were there to meet businesspeople from Vermont. A nice lady there said I had been recommended, and would I please send one of my demo tapes. I didn't have any demo tapes, so I said, 'Just talk to someone who's heard Danny, and if you still want me, I'm there.'

"And she said, 'Do you think they will understand Vermont humor?'

"So I said, 'Well, how bright are they?'"

Representative Gore's platform planks have always been common-sensical, usually tweaking the hypocrisy of politics. "Some politicians maintain that if you're old enough to die for your country, you're old enough to drink," Danny says. "I'm not sure when you're old enough to drink. But to die for your country, I think the minimum age should be fifty-five. That's when you've seen your children go through school, when you've enjoyed this great democracy—you may even have taken your grandchildren fishin'. So fifty-five is when you're old enough to die for your country. And I figure if we could get every country in the world to sit down and agree that we won't train any-one for war; we won't plan for war; we won't even *think* about war until the age of fifty-five, *then* we'd have peace."

Danny Gore (who occasionally receives visits from Norm Lewis) can be reached at P.O. Box 267, Danville, VT 05828, or by phone at (802) 684-2530.

# The Forked Stick Society

Good dowsers are known for their ability to find sources of underground water. The best dowsers are known for their ability to find lost items, track criminals, locate missing persons, and seek guidance of a more spiritual nature. Since its founding in 1958, in Danville, Vermont, the focus of the American Society of Dowsers has expanded from simply seeking water to include many uses and practices of dowsing. (For more information visit the American Society of Dowser's Web site at www.dowsers.org.)

—Chris Burns
*The Vermont Encyclopedia*

## The Audience Is in Vermont; the Performers Are in Canada

Derby Line

That would be the Haskell Opera House, with one minor qualification: As you will see by the black borderline when you visit, there actually are a few seats on the Canadian side. For fourteen seasons, QNEK (Quebec Northeast Kingdom) Productions has staged lively and varied musicals, revues, comedies, children's shows, and plays, all acted by its resident theater company.

Downstairs is the Haskell Free Library. Proceeds from the opera house assure that it is *really* free. "No rentals; no membership fees," says librarian Mary Roy. "We do have fines [for overdue books], though. A whopping two cents a day." (The librarians accept either

★ ★ ★ ★ ★ ★ ★ ★ ★ ★ ★ ★ ★ ★ ★ ★ ★ ★ ★ ★ ★ ★ ★ ★ ★ ★ ★ ★ ★ ★ ★ ★ ★ ★

U.S. or Canadian currency, on the grounds that things will pretty much even out at the end of the month.) By the way, a look at the black borderline on the library reading room floor will quickly tell you why this building is sometimes called "the only U.S. library with no books; the only Canadian theater with no stage." Modeled after the now defunct Boston Opera House, the neoclassical building was built to straddle the international border between Derby Line and what is now Stanstead, Quebec. American sawmill owner Carlos Haskell and his Canadian wife, Martha Stewart Haskell, wanted it to be used by people in both countries.

Did you guess that the line on the floor is an international boundary? Does the arrow help? (That's why we're here.)

Directions: Take exit 29 on Interstate 91; turn left over the bridge, go down the hill, and stop at the largest brick building in town, visible on the right, at 93 Caswell Avenue. The library is open year-round, Tuesday, Wednesday, and Friday, 10:00 a.m.–5:00 p.m., and Thursday, 10:00 a.m.–8:00 p.m. For more information visit www.haskellopera.org, or call the library at (802) 873-3022. The opera house's season runs from April to October. For concert tickets or information, call QNEK productions at (802) 334-2216 or visit www.qnek.com.

## The Bread and Puppet Theater

Glover

Such a cute name, is your first thought if you don't know better. But this is not your mama's down-home country theater, even if it is set in the countryside a couple of miles outside the village of Glover. True, the bread and the puppets are real enough. For the past forty years loaves of crusty sourdough bread have been baked and distributed with aioli (mayonnaise-garlic sauce) after each performance by director/founder Peter Schumann. "Theater is like bread," Schumann has said. "A necessity."

But Schumann, a German-born performance artist and sculptor, has not assembled his ensemble and the works they present for entertainment alone. He is here to inform, to protest—to provoke thought and action. This is pure political theater. Schumann's brand was born in 1963 during the Vietnam War, to give voice to frustrated protesters powerless to stop the fighting. It moved from New York to Vermont in 1970. Since then the troupe has performed all over the United States and in Europe, Latin America, and Asia.

I have read that Peter Schumann is viewed by some as a hero, and by others as an anarchist, a fact which I mention to Linda Elbow, the group's tour and business manager.

"What's the matter with being an anarchist?" says Linda. I'm on her side. This is what created both the United States and, at about the same time, the sovereign nation of Vermont. We agree that to some it is a loaded word, even the equivalent of *traitor*.

"Some people don't like to watch us," says Linda. "Where were we last week? . . . Oh, Glover Day! Every year we put on a performance for Glover Day, a show called *Runaway Pond*, commemorating a tragedy that happened here in 1810. Its bicentennial will be coming up soon. There had been a drought that year and not enough water was available to turn the wheel at the mill. Some local fellows went down to a nearby pond to dig a ditch that would let water flow

★ ★ ★ ★ ★ ★ ★ ★ ★ ★ ★ ★ ★ ★ ★ ★ ★ ★ ★ ★ ★ ★ ★ ★ ★ ★ ★ ★ ★ ★

**Home for Bread and Puppet's thousands of papier mâché masks, puppets, and props are two levels of a recently renovated 140-year-old hay barn, which also houses a bookshop.**

down to the mill 3 miles distant, which would in turn allow the mill wheel to turn, which would then solve the problem. Well, the hole they dug was in quicksand, and the whole earth gave way. It caused a massive flood from here to Newport [about 15 miles north]. So during the performance a woman walked by—I don't think she was local—and asked who was putting this on. When I told her she said, 'Oh, Bread and Puppet. They're garbage!'"

Sunday afternoons are primo for B&P Theater. Two hours earlier, a volunteer had directed me to one of the overflow parking lots about a quarter mile from the museum. Scores of cars line both sides of Route 122 and fill a couple of off-road lots. At a tour of the museum with thirty other guests, conducted by staff member Rose Friedman, I learn that the huge, 140-year-old hay barn housing the museum has undergone extensive reconstruction over the past year to neutralize its sinking slowly into the ground, and that the state has pitched in to help save this excellent example of agricultural architecture. On two levels of the barn are housed the thousands of papier-mâché and cardboard puppets—carved, painted, and molded—that have been used over the years, and that are resurrected as needed for present-day productions. Rose describes their context, as well as their functions.

Later Linda goes over the day's schedule. "After the circus we have a pageant. And after that we're doing an old street show called *Hallelujah*. And then after that a friend of ours from the Awareness Theater Company in Burlington is doing two presentations over there," she says, pointing to a building on the other side of the street. "Sundays are pretty full."

Bread and Puppet circuses incorporate political satire, dancing, music, parades, and sideshows that isolate one of the several themes for that particular circus, but also include material independent of that particular project's theme.

In addition to the Glover summer schedule, B&P maintains rigorous fall, winter, and spring tours dominated by visits to college campuses, centering on one region each season. Their most recent fall schedule included colleges, high schools, and communities in North Carolina, Georgia, and Virginia, winding up in New York City during late November and December for Divine Reality Circus and Pageant performances over the holidays. The international schedule for any given year could be as diverse as, say, Haiti, Italy, and Canada.

Directions: The theater is south of Glover Village about 1 mile on Route 122, at 753 Heights Road. During July and August the troupe performs on the Glover grounds Friday evenings and Sunday afternoons. There usually is a mid- to late-June celebration of the museum opening, and afternoon performances in October, the annual political leaf peeping. Performances are free, but donations are welcome. The museum is open June through October, 10:00 a.m. to 5:00 p.m. daily. No admission required, but donations are encouraged. Call (802) 525-1271 for details or visit www.breadandpuppet.org.

★ ★ ★ ★ ★ ★ ★ ★ ★ ★ ★ ★ ★ ★ ★ ★ ★ ★ ★ ★ ★ ★ ★ ★ ★ ★ ★ ★ ★ ★ ★ ★

### Brutal Raid on an Abenaki Village
Granby

On a mountaintop just beyond a log house a mile north of Granby, a 10-foot-by-12-foot split-rail-fenced cemetery holds two graves, each graced with a small American flag. Nearby, a granite bench awaits the rare visitor who comes to pay homage.

No way would I have found this place without the help of Joe Benning, a Lyndonville attorney with an interest in colonial history, who has kindly taken the afternoon off to show me the grave sites and give me a tour of the area. "This is the final resting place of two of the famed Rogers' Rangers," says Joe. A plaque inside the split rail fence verifies this.

Major Robert Rogers was a New Hampshire farmer recruited in 1755 by the British for service in the French and Indian War. This was back in the days when New York occupied the territory that is now Vermont, and New Hampshire claimed it as well. In 1759 Rogers was ordered by British general Jeffrey Amherst to leave Crown Point, New York, and attack the Abenaki village of Odanak, on the Saint Francis River in Canada. This was a revenge attack, in retaliation for the Abenaki's longtime alliance with the French, and for a recent raid on a retreating British unit.

The Abenaki at Odanak (also called Saint Francis) had been celebrating an excellent hunting and gathering harvest that fall, dancing and feasting well into the night. The main body of Rogers's unit—about 150 men—waited 3 miles from the village while two scouts kept watch. About a half hour before dawn, after the entire village had retired, Rogers and his men attacked. Three hours later, up to 200 men, women, and children were dead, and smoking ruins were all that remained of nearly all the sixty or more frame houses and a Jesuit mission church. Only about one hundred Abenaki are thought to have survived.

About a week after their retreat from Odanak, the Rangers broke into small groups somewhere near Lake Memphremagog on the U.S.-

Canadian border. Their destination was
Fort Number 4, at Charles-
town, New Hampshire, on
the Connecticut River. At
least three groups of Rangers came down through
what is now the Northeast
Kingdom. Many of them
had little room for food in
their packs, having looted
the church in Odanak of
silver-plated copper chan-
deliers, "massive" golden
candlesticks, and a solid
silver statuette of Our Lady
of Chartres inlaid with a ruby
"as big as an eyeball." Other
sources also mention bags of silver and gold coins.

The Rangers buried at this hilltop site were part of a raiding party on an Canadian Abenaki village in 1758.

But here's where the stories get confusing. Most agree that as
hunger took its toll, the men gradually discarded their plunder, most
marking their hiding places for retrieval later. The two soldiers who
got as far as Granby, however, just 20 miles from the Connecticut
River, are said to have been killed either by wolves who disputed their
ownership of a killed moose, or by Abenaki who trailed and finally
caught up with them.

"In either case," says Joe Benning, "I don't know how you could
prove it at this late date without exhuming the remains."

Directions: To reach the grave sites, take I-91 exit 23; then travel on
U.S. Route 5 through Lyndonville approximately 2 miles to Route 114.
Then go another 3 miles to a fork at which Route 114 bears left, and
Victory Road (not marked) goes right. Take the right. Go another 3
miles to Granby, and take the first left, Porrell Road. At the top of the
mountain, just past a log house, are the fenced grave sites on the left.

★ ★ ★ ★ ★ ★ ★ ★ ★ ★ ★ ★ ★ ★ ★ ★ ★ ★ ★ ★ ★ ★ ★ ★ ★ ★ ★ ★ ★ ★ ★ ★ ★

### And the Best New England Diner Is . . . *Miss Lyndonville!*

Lyndonville

Let's start with breakfast. If words such as *cholesterol* or *carbohydrates* are not in your working vocabulary, may I suggest the country-fried steak breakfast: breaded beefsteak with country gravy, home fries, two eggs "your way," and homemade toast. Or perhaps the stuffed French toast. Delicious, and hats off to the manager—or maybe it was the chef—who easily could have named this concoction "a grilled double orange marmalade and cream cheese sandwich (yes, on four slices of white bread), with maple syrup, bananas, and pecans." Could have, that is, if sales were no object.

But let's say you bring some resolve to the table and are not one of the weak-kneed or undisciplined eaters among us. Fine. Then you'll probably be eating at home, because restaurant breakfasts are about indulging oneself. But if not, there are many modest and healthy options for those occasions when you are accompanying a food-focused friend.

Now, what's for lunch? Actually, I had to leave right after breakfast but saw on the menu a wide selection of nutritious soups, salads, and sandwiches. Still, I think it's the service as much as the food that has caused publications such as *Vermont Life, Interstate Gourmet,* and *A Yankee Notebook* to rave about Miss Lyndonville Diner and rank her above Miss Everybody Else. At the counter Amy, Kat, and Kim were quick, efficient, and attentive, never letting my coffee fall below the half-cup mark. I was able to eat only half of my stuffed French toast (I know, but it was Amy's personal favorite; I *had* to sample it) and asked to take the rest with me. The uneaten half returned wrapped and covered, along with a fresh napkin, plastic knife and fork, and a container of fresh coffee (no charge). At that point Amy did not know I'd be writing about the diner. I told her only after she asked why I wanted to take a menu with me.

"[It's] . . . like stepping through a time warp," wrote *A Yankee Notebook,* "into an America we thought had disappeared."

Directions: To reach the Miss Lyndonville Diner, take I-91 exit 23, and then head north on U.S. Route 5. The diner is approximately 1 mile toward Lyndonville, on the right, at 686 Broad Street. Hours vary by day of the week, so for the best information call (802) 626-9890.

## Kingdom County Productions—Hello to Vollywood!
Peacham

Vermont's Northeast Kingdom is the film capital of northern New England. In addition to feature films and documentaries, it offers an additional bonus, or perhaps legacy. Whatever you call it, Bess O'Brien and Jay Craven have found a way to seed, nurture, and harvest a continual crop of formative stage and screen pros, behind and in front of both camera and proscenium. True, this is not the principal mission at Kingdom County Productions, but it is an organic outgrowth.

Bess gives me an example one fall afternoon as we sit on a side porch of the couple's Peacham home, overlooking a wide swath of the Connecticut River valley. (Jay is in Africa and Asia, part of a cultural exchange on behalf of the State Department and the National Endowment of the Arts, talking to independent filmmakers about his newest film, *Disappearance.*)

"About five years ago, Blue Cross/Blue Shield of Vermont asked me to create a project based on the lives of Vermont teenagers—the hook being the health of kids in the state," says Bess, working on a late lunch of cheese and crackers. "I came up with the idea of an original musical, along the lines of *Fame.* We spent about eight months all over Vermont, using workshops to learn about the lives of kids from all walks of life. Then we put together a script based on the kids we had met."

Bess and coproducer/cowriter Abby Paige then brought in a number of talented teenagers to write the original music. The finished piece, a theater production called *Voices,* toured in thirteen towns all over Vermont. It was a big sensation, to the extent that Bess turned it into a screenplay and an independent film under the Kingdom County

★ ★ ★ ★ ★ ★ ★ ★ ★ ★ ★ ★ ★ ★ ★ ★ ★ ★ ★ ★ ★ ★ ★ ★ ★ ★ ★ ★ ★ ★ ★ ★

Bess O'Brien and Jay Craven examine a film script—a good one, from the looks of them—at their home in Peacham.

Productions (KCP) banner. A more extended tour of the film—to fifty towns in Vermont—will be followed by submissions to international film festivals and a tour of New England.

"Now I'm editing that film with an editor I worked with on one of my documentaries. She's a student of Jay's, who also teaches at Marlboro College. She graduated years ago and has worked her way up. Her name is Carrie Sterr, and she's terrific. A lot of Jay's students who graduate from Marlboro we end up hiring through the years.

"For *Voices* this summer, we used a lot of interns—film students from Marlboro, Burlington College, Keene State—so they got a chance to work with mentors, not getting paid, but learning a lot. So it's a great thing for their résumés and they get a lot of experience." To bring it full circle, Carrie served as film-editing mentor to the students interested in her chosen field.

The other option KCP has for young people interested in a film career is its Fledgling Films arm, organized in 1997 to give young people hands-on experience in media arts production. One Fledgling student directed an off-Broadway play last summer and spent the fall semester shooting two films. Another graduate of the Fledgling Summer Institute started his own youth film festival.

Despite minuscule budgets compared to those at Hollywood-studio level—that happens to be what KCP can afford, after all—the studio attracts such top-dollar talent as Rip Torn, Martin Sheen, Michael J. Fox, Geneviève Bujold, and Kris Kristofferson.

"Michael J. Fox was terrific," says Bess. "He was living in Vermont at the time, and it was one of those things—we knew the guy who was working on his house. He told Michael there were filmmakers in the Northeast Kingdom who wanted to meet him." Fox watched *High Water,* was impressed, met Jay and Bess, and agreed to be in *Where the Rivers Flow North,* which also starred Rip Torn and Tantoo Cardinal.

"Because he was shooting another movie in Canada at the time, it was difficult trying to get through to his manager. For managers and agents it's all about the money, and protecting their clients from all the people who want them to do every project in the world. But you never know. With Kris we *did* go through his agent, and it worked out. Kris called here one day out of the blue and read the script [for *Disappearances*] and loved it. He said, 'I'm committed to this project for however long it takes.' It took five years from that phone call to get the money together. But he hung in there."

So why do stars of this caliber work with KCP for so little money, comparatively?

"I think they do it because a lot of the roles they are asked to do give them a lot of money but aren't challenging to them. I think Kris, for example, although he does a lot of commercial work, saw this as a terrific role to play as an older man. In an independent film you can take more risks, and it's not all about the money. Plus Jay's a fine director and the scripts are really strong.

"Ours are rural films with minimal national distribution power. They're like vaudeville. We make them and then we tour them from town to town. Not that it will make anyone a lot of money, but

★ ★ ★ ★ ★ ★ ★ ★ ★ ★ ★ ★ ★ ★ ★ ★ ★ ★ ★ ★ ★ ★ ★ ★ ★ ★ ★ ★

that it's a good thing to do, enriches the region, and disseminates a film to its own culture in a way that reflects Vermont and otherwise would not be out there."

For a detailed look at the history of Kingdom County Productions, its critically acclaimed films, and its current and upcoming activities, see www.kingdomcounty.com. To learn more about the *Voices* project, go to www.bcbsvt.com/voices.

### Vermont Educator, Legislator, and Historian without Peer
Saint Johnsbury

"No, not there. To the right. Down one shelf. Yes. There it is."

I'm in Graham Newell's St. Johnsbury study on a sunny Sunday September afternoon. He is sharing a little historical gossip and directing me to Calvin Coolidge's autobiography from his armchair across the room. Graham, 92, uses a walker to get around but still teaches intermediate Latin in his home three times weekly to a dozen St. Johnsbury Academy students.

Coolidge was rejected at Amherst, Graham tells me, because the academic standards at his school, Black River Academy, were too low. But Amherst's administrators agreed that

Nine months after this photo was taken, Graham Newell died at 92. Colleagues admired his "bear-trap mind." Graham lauded his students' triumphs and sublimated his own.

if Coolidge came to St. Johnsbury Academy and made decent grades for a year, they would admit him.

Graham asks me to read the Coolidge account: After a few weeks in the winter at my old school, I went to St. Johnsbury Academy for the spring term. Its principal was Dr. Putney . . . a very exact scholar and an excellent disciplinarian. He readily gave me a certificate entitling me to enter Amherst without further examination, which he would never have done if he had not been convinced I was a proficient student."

"Oh, that's Coolidge for you," says Graham, chortling.

Back to the printed account: "[Dr. Putney's] endorsement of [my work] . . . showed that Black River Academy was not without some merit."

"When he wrote this thirty years later, though," says Graham with obvious glee, "Black River Academy was flourishing. So you can see he doesn't tell you the whole story—that Black River Academy couldn't get him into Amherst!"

Graham Newell is seventh-generation Saint Johnsbury, and the town's honorary ambassador. "People send people who move here to me when they want to quickly know the history of our town." He shows me the genealogical cheat sheet he has prepared for such occurrences. "You've got to memorize the names of the three Fairbanks brothers at the top there: Thaddeus, inventor of the scale; Erastus, governor twice of Vermont; and their brother, Joseph, who died young but had one son who built the house next to me, and who wrote a history of the town of Saint Johnsbury."

Graham started teaching English, Latin, and then history at Saint Johnsbury Academy after graduating from the University of Chicago in 1938. (He later returned for his master's degree in Latin and completed course work for his Ph.D.) In 1953 Newell ran successfully for the Vermont legislature and served in both the house and senate for twenty-six years—twenty of them as chairman of the senate education committee—while maintaining his position as head of the history

department at Lyndon State College. Because the legislature didn't meet on Mondays, Graham conducted classes on campus those days. On Wednesdays and Fridays he climbed up to the "crow's nest" of the Capitol Dome in Montpelier and communicated with his history students through a long-distance telephone hookup called a telelecture. An assistant at Lyndon State transmitted student questions back to Graham. As a legislator Graham is proudest of two bills he wrote and prodded to passage in the late 1950s. The Fair Dismissal for Teachers bill guarantees that no teacher can be fired without a hearing. His Special Education bill was the first legislation nationwide to establish a public school curriculum, grades K–12, for students with special needs. Graham voted as an "Aiken Republican," the liberal wing of the party, but today considers himself an Independent.

In 1962 Graham recalls being summoned from the Senate floor for a call from the White House. "President Kennedy's right-hand man told me the President had just appointed me a member of the Advisory Commission on Intergovernmental Relations. The Commission consisted—as it does today—of two members of every body of government at national, state, county, and municipal levels–about 24 members in all. Graham, one of two state legislators selected nationwide, met with his colleagues once a month in Washington. "Senator Sam Ervin [later Chairman of the Watergate Commission] was chairman of the entire commission, and I got to know him very well. In October 1963 we were told that JFK had invited us to meet with him at the White House for our December 1 meeting. One month later he was dead. That was the most tragic of my few brushes with what I call fame.

"At the moment," says Graham, "I'm disposing of a lot of my books and historical documents. I have hundreds, going back to the eighteenth century. I thought of giving them to the University of Vermont. I received an honorary doctorate there a couple of years ago. The Vermont Historical Society was a possibility, as well. I was president there from 1964 to 1969. But I've decided that everything will go across the street to the Newell Collection, in the academy's archive room."

Only fitting, it seems, that one of the rare *living* icons to have a building named for him—Newell Hall, in this case—would trust his most prized possessions to an institution that in turn values him so highly.

Directions: Take exit 20 on I-91. At the end of the exit ramp, turn right, and take the next left up the hill. When the road levels out, you will be on Main Street and at the Saint Johnsbury Academy campus. For more information visit www.stjohnsburyacademy.org.

## 13,555 Beetles and Butterflies Died for This Artistic Experiment
Saint Johnsbury

Given the title of this book, you shouldn't be surprised that we've taken the low road here. The Fairbanks Museum "bug art" exhibit described a few paragraphs from now, however, is not representative of the high standard maintained elsewhere in the building.

We begin by reintroducing Erastus Fairbanks from the previous entry, whose son Franklin founded the Fairbanks Museum. Franklin Fairbanks, who became president of the scale company started by his uncle Thaddeus, wanted to give something back to the community. What better gift than a three-level museum that he could seed with exhibits from his own vast personal collection, which he called his "cabinet of curiosities." Our kind of guy! It became a reality in 1889. Following is a brief tour.

*Lower Floor*. The Fairbanks Museum and Planetarium (its full name) has maintained a weather observation site in its basement ever since 1894, largely because Franklin Fairbanks kept meticulous weather records in his Saint Johnsbury home. It seemed natural for him to make the weather bureau—and ultimately the planetarium—a permanent part of the museum.

Meteorologists Mark Breen and Steve Maleski have broadcast eight or more daily weather forecasts over Vermont Public Radio since 1981. Their comprehensive analyses go far beyond customary "cloudy today, sunny tomorrow" TV two-minute reports. "Our focus is basically the North American continent and surrounding areas," says Breen, "because it directly impacts [Vermont] weather. A storm track out in the Pacific during the typhoon season, for example, has an effect on storms that eventually reach Alaska, which in turn affects the weather pattern across North America. Covering that broad an area encompasses most of the factors that affect us five or six days from now, which we discuss in a general sense. Then we look in more detail at regions closer to us, to talk about the impact over the next forty-eight hours."

"Completed in 1897," reads the plaque. "Honoring the Articles of Confederation and perpetual union created in 1777. This work contains 13,555 beetles and butterflies."

As you might also guess, there is a tribute to the Fairbanks platform scale that made all of this possible. It's on display just a few feet down from the Snowflake Bentley exhibit, courtesy of the museum's founder's uncle Thaddeus, who not only invented it but distributed it worldwide, to China, Russia, Cuba, India, and much of Europe. By 1897 the company held 113 patents for inventions and improvements in weighing.

*Main Floor.* The ground floor is dominated by 75,000 mounted birds, reptiles, mammals, and fish. Franklin was also an amateur naturalist, and some of the birds he shot became part of the extensive "Birds and Animals of the World" display. Taxidermist William Balch did the stuffing and mounting, as well as some of the shooting. Two pair of now-extinct passenger pigeons are included, as well as a collection of 131 species of hummingbirds, thought to be the largest such collection in North America.

*Upper Level.* Now. Ah yes, the bug art. The perpetrator of these works is John Hampson, who at one time worked as a mechanical engineer for Thomas Edison in New Jersey and in his spare time arranged dead insects into shapes depicting historical events. The one that took 13,555 butterflies and beetles (and several years) to complete was a representation of Old Glory honoring the Articles of Confederation. Others include *Abraham Lincoln's Proclamation of Freedom, General Pershing on His Horse,* and *Washington Bidding His Generals Goodby.* When Hampson died, his daughter trolled a num-

## Trivia

**Somebody had to photograph the first snowflake:** *quoted from the exhibit plaque at Saint Johnsbury's Fairbanks Museum.* **Wilson "Snowflake" Bentley was a Vermont treasure, as unique as the snow crystals he captured as microphotographs. A self-educated farmer from Jericho, he invented the process of microphotography using a microscope and camera. He went on to capture over 5,000 images of snow crystals from 1885 until his death in 1931. In addition, he studied formations of frost, dew, and raindrops in great detail. He also conducted some of the first research in cloud physics.**

★ ★ ★ ★ ★ ★ ★ ★ ★ ★ ★ ★ ★ ★ ★ ★ ★ ★ ★ ★ ★ ★ ★ ★ ★ ★ ★

ber of museums pleading for bug-art perpetuity, with the Fairbanks finally agreeing to display the nine works. The upper level (balcony) also leads to the planetarium.

Directions: Take I-91 exit 20 (U.S. Route 5 /Railroad Street) and go north to Main Street. Go left up the hill 2 blocks beyond the stop sign. The museum is on the right, at 1302 Main. Museum hours and planetarium showings vary by season. For more information call (802) 748-2372, or better yet, visit the museum's Web site at www .fairbanksmuseum.org, where a virtual tour is even available, though the real thing is much better.

# 9

# Upper Champlain Valley

**Only about 110** *miles long and 12 miles wide, most folks wouldn't think to call Lake Champlain "great." Yet for one week it came close to achieving legislative renown. The intent was simply to make Vermont schools eligible to receive "Sea Grant funding" by adding Lake Champlain to the list of Great Lakes already being funded. Instead, some midwesterners were outraged. A* New York Times *story claimed that Vermont senator Patrick Leahy had slipped seven additional words into the bill: "The term Great Lakes includes Lake Champlain." We got us a brouhaha! But it all turned out well, as you'll see.*

*Senator Leahy also had a hand in establishing ECHO Lake Aquarium and Science Center—Vermont's best location to study "Ecology, Culture, History, and Opportunity." But it was* Country Home *magazine that named Burlington tops among all U.S. cities for "Best Green Places."*

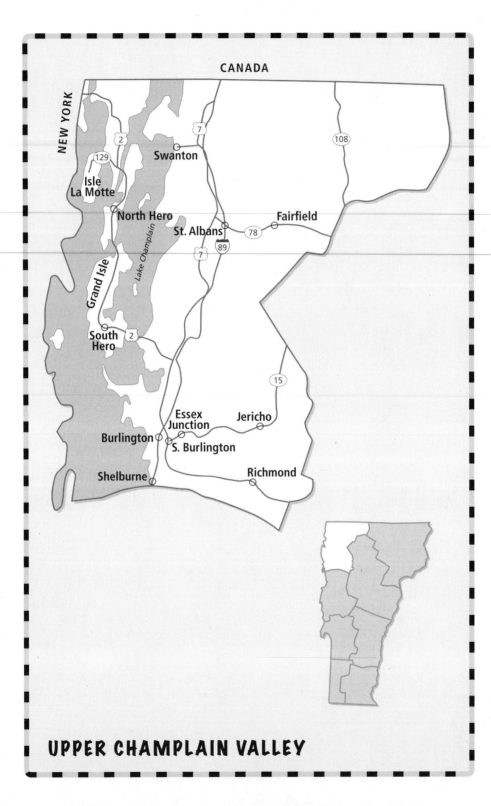

UPPER CHAMPLAIN VALLEY

✱ ✱ ✱ ✱ ✱ ✱ ✱ ✱ ✱ ✱ ✱ ✱ ✱ ✱ ✱ ✱ ✱ ✱ ✱ ✱ ✱ ✱ ✱ ✱ ✱ ✱ ✱ ✱ ✱ ✱ ✱ ✱ ✱ ✱ ✱ ✱ ✱

### ECHO . . . ECHO . . . ECHO . . . Lake Aquarium and Science Center
Burlington

Just before you set foot in ECHO, a fine mist sprayed between slabs of lake slate bathes the air on both sides of the two-story glass entrance. I saw dancing rainbows, but that can't always happen, can it? Even if not, it sure is a good mood-setter.

This estimable establishment is called "ECHO Lake Aquarium and Science Center at the Leahy Center for Lake Champlain." ECHO stands for ecology, culture, history, and opportunity—a mouthful that is also quite accurate. It is named in honor of Vermont's U.S. senator Patrick Leahy and his wife, Marcelle. Senator Leahy raised $7.5 million—over half the building's total cost—from three federal agencies to build the waterfront center.

"All of the content and all of exhibits work together," says Julie Silverman, director of New (as in innovative, visionary ideas). "In 1995 we took over an old naval reserve building that was on this site. We stayed there for six years until plans for the new building were in place. Two years later, in 2003, we moved in.

"Anything we could salvage from the old building, we did. The boards we're standing on are Douglas fir timbers from the old building, replaned, remilled, and put in as decking." This example of reclamation is but one of dozens of ecological decisions that led to ECHO being the first Vermont building certified by the U.S. Green Building Council the year it opened. Other criteria for this rating include energy use and renewal, environmental impact, and waste management and recycling.

As to the last of these, come with me into the men's room, an interactive exhibit unto itself. The sign above the toilet reads: YOU DECIDE. CHOOSE WISELY TO HELP CONSERVE WATER, A SCARCE RESOURCE.

Left-button instructions: PUSH THE "ONE-HALF FLUSH" BUTTON TO USE ONLY .8 OF A GALLON OF WATER. Right-button instructions: PUSH THE "WHOLE-FLUSH" BUTTON TO USE 1.6 GALLONS OF WATER. Underneath the buttons a

Look at that cute little guy saying "come on in!" One passerby was heard to say as she looked at the window painting: "I think the drawing is fabulous. It just looks airy and inviting."

sign reads: ECHOS'S WATER SAVINGS FOR SINKS, TOILETS, AND URINALS EXCEEDS THE U.S. ENERGY POLICY ACT BY 36 PERCENT.

There is one other urinal option, completely hygienic and requiring the use of no water at all. As the sign says: By using this touch-free system, you are helping the environment to conserve an average of 40,000 gallons of fresh water per urinal per year. How do they do that? Details online at www.falconwaterfree.com.

The ECHO Green Lantern Team, a collection of staff and volunteers, are watchdogs who look at ways to improve the inner workings of the operation on a continuing basis, including recycling, cleaning products, purchasing, and paper use. (Memo to Green Lantern Team: This may not be within your purview, but finding a way to make the men's room a part-time, mutual-embarrassment-and-gender-free exhibit would be a challenge worth consideration.)

Julie sums up the philosophy behind the many attractions at ECHO, including the more than seventy species of live fish, amphibians, and reptiles. "We are very much place based," she says. "Most of the content and exhibits are about the Lake Champlain basin. We give people an opportunity to see species they would never see otherwise—the sturgeon, for example, because that type of historic animal has been around as long as the dinosaurs."

According to Julie, that information usually elicits one of two follow-up questions, particularly from school groups: "*That* lives in Lake Champlain?" or "That fish is as old as a dinosaur?"

"Yes," of course, is the answer to the first question. As to the second, guides proclaim, usually on a daily basis, "No, we're not talking about *that particular sturgeon*. We're saying the sturgeon species has been around as long as the dinosaurs!"

The sturgeon and other major fish exhibits are downstairs in the under-the-lake exhibit. Frogs, turtles, newts, and other aboveground creatures live upstairs.

Allow plenty of time. Trying to cover the wealth of information and surprises available to ECHO visitors in a single day is overly ambitious. Try planning your trip in advance by reviewing the Web site.

Directions: Enter Burlington on U.S. Route 2, which becomes Main Street. Turn north onto Battery Street. Drive 1 block and take a left at the light onto College Street. ECHO is located at the bottom of College Street on the waterfront. Hours vary by season and special exhibits change frequently, so check ahead. For more information visit www.echovermont.org or call (877) ECHOFUN.

# Best of the "Best Green Places"

Attention, everyone. This just in: *Country Home* magazine has announced the results of its first "Best Green Places" Survey, rating U.S. cities on the basis of air and watershed quality, mass transit use, power use, and number of organic producers and farmers' markets. Of the 379 metropolitan areas listed, Burlington, Vermont, was rated number one.

Burlington received high marks for:

- A compost facility that collects food scraps from restaurants and supermarkets and sells them to farmers and gardeners.

- Its sixteen farmers' markets, five organic producers, and three food co-ops.

- The 12.3 percent of its commuters who carpool, the 5.6 percent of its workforce that walk to work, and the 4.6 percent who work at home.

Top rankings from other adjacent states among the 379 listed:

| | |
|---|---|
| Ithaca, New York | 2 |
| Springfield, Massachusetts | 4 |
| Portland, Maine | 34 |
| Rockingham County-Strafford County, New Hampshire | 187 |

Congratulations to all green-worthy participants!

## Lake Champlain—Honorary Great Lake for a Week
Burlington

On March 5, 1998, President Bill Clinton signed Senate Bill 927, written primarily to reauthorize the Sea Grant Program, which deals with the study of environmental issues concerning states that border the Great Lakes and states with coastlines. This legislation incidentally recognized Lake Champlain as the nation's sixth Great Lake, along with Lakes Superior, Ontario, Michigan, Erie, and Huron, for purposes of projects and funding. One week later, the Great Lakes Commission (a binational U.S. and state agency dedicated to promoting a healthy environment for the Great Lakes–Saint Lawrence region) decreed that Lake Champlain was no longer a Great Lake. What happened?

During that week—and for months thereafter—the contention was that Senator Patrick Leahy was trying to pull a fast one. The American Geological Institute referred to an amendment by Senator Leahy "to include Lake Champlain as one of the Great Lakes . . . in order for schools in Vermont to receive Sea Grant funding." A *New York Times* story claimed that Senator Leahy slipped seven words into the bill: "'The term Great Lakes includes Lake Champlain'—and thus unleashed a storm of protest in the Middle West."

Ohio senator John Glenn adapted a quote from an earlier Lloyd Bentsen–Dan Quayle vice presidential debate: "I know the Great Lakes. I've traveled to the Great Lakes. And Lake Champlain is not one of the Great Lakes."

The only accurate part of these accusations was that the senator did indeed want the University of Vermont to be able to compete for National Sea Grant College status. "The arguments for [Lake Champlain] being very similar [to the Great Lakes] in almost all regards except total area is pretty strong," said Dr. Larry Forcier, director of the Lake Champlain Sea Grant program at the University of Vermont.

But even so, Senator Leahy never requested that Lake Champlain be added as the sixth Great Lake, only that it be eligible for Sea

★ ★ ★ ★ ★ ★ ★ ★ ★ ★ ★ ★ ★ ★ ★ ★ ★ ★ ★ ★ ★ ★ ★ ★ ★ ★ ★ ★

Grant money. Bob Paquin, a Vermont aide to Senator Leahy, recalls it this way: "The words Senator Leahy added to the bill after the words 'shall include the Great Lakes' were '[comma] and Lake Champlain.' But agencies affected by the legislation are customarily invited to comment on bill language, and in this case it was the National Oceanic and Atmospheric Administration. NOAA officials asked that Senator Leahy's wording be changed to include Lake Champlain in the definition of the Great Lakes watershed."

Paquin agrees with Larry Forcier regarding Lake Champlain's qualifications for receiving Sea Grant funding. "Among scientists there's no debate on the hydrology," he said. "We are part of the Great Lakes–Saint Lawrence system. So including the canal system—Champlain, Hudson River, and Erie—in terms of invasive species, for example, whatever they get, we get."

So the Leahy team went along with that language because it accomplished its goal. But then a Midwest news organization picked up an article in the *Burlington, Vermont, Free Press* about the Sea Grant funding provision and the reworked NOAA language, and in one day it was all over the country that Lake Champlain had been declared a Great Lake. Reporters searched their Rolodexes to find geologists for interviews about the controversy.

Midwestern lawmakers, when asked back home whether they had been asleep at the switch, reacted with indignation. With a bit of egg on its face, the Michigan-based

These Lake Champlain swimmers don't care whether they're in a Great Lake. They simply know it's a great lake.

Great Lakes Commission on March 11 opposed the designation of Lake Champlain as a "Great Lake." Within days the Senate unanimously passed Leahy's compromise, adding Lake Champlain to Sea Grant eligibility status, and listing it as "among the Great Lakes natural resources."

The Sea Grant people were delighted with the publicity. Senator Leahy and his staff accomplished their mission. And the State University of New York at Plattsburgh was a benefactor as well, happy to join the Sea Grant team by virtue of its location on the west side of Lake Champlain.

"The Senator found the whole sequence amusing," said Bob Paquin. "We like to say that Lake Champlain is still 'great' to us—and after all, if you take 1776 into account, it is this country's *first* great lake." In any case, scientists on both sides of the lake will now be able to conduct research to help solve its problems, eradicating the zebra mussel and other invasive species, for example, which affect the five other Great Lakes, as well.

## Cultural Magnet for a Community
Burlington

Back in 1930 John J. Flynn built the Flynn Theatre strictly for vaudeville. With its huge proscenium arch—largest in the state—future backstage expansion definitely was an option. In the interim the Golden Age of Hollywood came calling, which meant adapting that proscenium to accommodate a fixed screen for the first of the talkies. For a brief time thereafter, a movable screen accommodated both film and performance art. Then the Flynn made its complete break. Despite a relatively low population base, new ownership counted on growing community interest to support its total commitment to live theater, music, and dance. After a complete renovation in 1981, the Flynn Center for the Performing Arts was born. Its inaugural concert in an all-live-all-the-time format included the Vermont Symphony Orchestra and a number of area artists.

★ ★ ★ ★ ★ ★ ★ ★ ★ ★ ★ ★ ★ ★ ★ ★ ★ ★ ★ ★ ★ ★ ★ ★ ★ ★ ★ ★ ★ ★

Since that time several additional renovations have made the Flynn the region's leading performance center, now run by local community leaders as a nonprofit organization. It is recognized internationally (Canada is only an hour away) for its artistic activities, its superb technical capacity, and its world-class presentations. In any given month the main stage hosts road companies from Japan to Nebraska, and performances are often sold out well before opening night.

Throughout its frequent makeovers the physical plant's art deco integrity has been scrupulously preserved. On a tour of the house, facilities director Jack Galt points out the meticulous application of a thin line of gold paint to the wrought iron railings. It enhances a three-dimensional effect that visitors will appreciate, if only subconsciously.

What separates the Flynn from most other commercial live-performance theaters, though, is the extent of its community outreach, which takes several forms. There are performing arts classes, for example, embracing an array of acting, dance, and music classes for one-year-olds, ninety-year-olds, and all in between. There's voice for teens and adults, ballet, directing for the stage, jazz combo, stand-up comedy, hip-hop, rhythm tap, junior creative dance, and a dozen more. Also scheduled are one-time evening and weekend workshops and programs to help educators improve their creative arts teaching skills.

In 1997 the Flynn was part of a gala community fund-raising bash, in concert with the legendary Vermont rock band Phish and entrepreneurs Ben Cohen and Jerry Greenfield—better known as the founders of Ben & Jerry's ice cream. B&J had created a flavor called Phish Food in honor of the band (later spun off as the popular chocolate-covered ice cream bar Phish Sticks). To simultaneously kick off the release of this ice cream flavor and to validate the environmental awareness of both B&J and the band, 100 percent of the royalties from the license of Phish Food were funneled into Waterwheel, the band's nonprofit organization. Through Waterwheel, all such funds are used to clean up the Lake Champlain watershed from industrial, urban, and agricultural runoff. The concert was a sellout.

Directions: Coming in on U.S. Route 2, which turns into Main Street, the Flynn Center is at 153 Main, just west of the Burlington City Hall. For more information about the center or for tickets, visit www.flynncenter.org, or call (802) 86-FLYNN.

## A 25,000-Mile, in-State Stroll

Essex Junction

*The 251 Club Wayfarer* is a newsletter for Vermonters intent on visiting all 251 of the state's towns and cities. *Wayfarer* editor Bill Rockford gave me a paragraph in one edition to ask members about their unusual experiences. One response stood out by far.

Dr. Edward Keenan had never set out to log all 251 Vermont communities. Only after he received a gift membership did he and his wife begin attending meetings. Following are a few of Dr. Keenan's recollections:

Photo courtesy *Burlington Free Press*

Ione Keenan meets up with husband, Ed, who has just completed a 78-mile, 20-hour walk from Bradford to Burlington, raising $10,000 for the Fanny Allen Hospital (ca. 1975).

★ ★ ★ ★ ★ ★ ★ ★ ★ ★ ★ ★ ★ ★ ★ ★ ★ ★ ★ ★ ★ ★ ★ ★ ★ ★ ★ ★

"Many of my early long walks had to do with the American Lung Association's annual 100-mile Bike Treks. I would start about 2 a.m., many miles before the first cyclists passed me. My longest one-day walk was 89 miles, completed in 23 hours, 20 minutes. My longest multi-day walk started at the Massachusetts border and ended at the Canadian border four days later.

"I took seats out of my van to convert it to a mobile home. By careful planning I mapped out circle routes to begin and end where the van was parked. On a 78-mile walk from Bradford to Burlington to benefit the Fanny Allen Hospital, one of the nuns walked with me from the airport to the waterfront.

"I will never forget the interesting and caring folks I met along the way. People filled me in on points of interest in their town. Many asked me in for tea, or to rest. One family took me to a church supper; another gentleman invited me to his restaurant for dinner. One bitterly cold day a man came out with his pickup truck twice to be sure I was all right. And my appearance was not all that reassuring! I wore old, comfortable clothing and had not always shaved that morning. Also, because I can't stand to see clutter along the road, I was always carrying a sack or two of beer cans and bottles. When the sacks got too heavy I would stash them in the woods and return later in the van to pick them up.

"I met many interesting—and sometimes scary—two- and four-footed critters along the way, as well. One morning on a dead-end dirt road I heard a muffled growling. Beneath the exposed roots of a tree overhanging the river bank, a fisher cat was devouring—I couldn't tell what, maybe a rodent or a fish. Fisher cats are ferocious and combative, with long curved claws and vicious teeth. I hastily gave him a wide berth, dreading that I would have to retrace my steps in a few minutes. Fortunately he was gone when I returned.

"Another day I came upon a large she-bear rooting around in an abandoned garden. I stood stock still, but suddenly she detected my scent and reared up on her hind legs. We stared at each other for a few long moments. Then she dropped down on all fours and ambled across the road in front of me, followed by a yearling cub that I saw for the first time. One bitter cold day, a chickadee lit on the edge of my hood, at the level of my glasses. I spoke softly to her and she stayed for a few seconds; then was gone as quickly as she had come.

"It was not until I finished walking our two southernmost counties that I realized I was the first 251 Club member ever to have walked in all the towns. On November 7, 1999, I reached my goal of having walked every road in the state of Vermont–except for the interstates, on which pedestrians are prohibited. My mileage totaled 25,000.

"I never set out to earn my "unique-plus" membership, but on the road of life it is rare to set out for the destination we eventually reach."

—By Edward A. Keenan Jr., M.D.,
as told to Ione Lacy Keenan

## Is He One of Us, or Not?

Fairfield

If twenty-first president Chester A. Arthur were alive today, he'd have a little 'splainin' to do.

"Sir," one might ask, "were you legally entitled to become president? You say you were born in Fairfield, Vermont. Yet no birth certificate has been found to indicate that you were not in fact born just over the border in Canada."

Or "Sir, you said throughout your lifetime that you

President Chester A. Arthur's modest birthplace in Fairfield.

★ ★ ★ ★ ★ ★ ★ ★ ★ ★ ★ ★ ★ ★ ★ ★ ★ ★ ★ ★ ★ ★ ★ ★ ★ ★ ★ ★ ★ ★ ★

were born in 1829, but the year inscribed on your gravestone is 1830."

Or even "Sir, it is said that you secluded yourself in the White House for two and one-half months after President James A. Garfield was shot and before he died. It is said the reason for this is that you knew many people thought you had something to do with his assassination. What do you say in answer to this charge, sir?"

It seems a pretty lucky thing that most of us have only one life to live.

President Arthur could be asked still other questions: Why no vice president? Why no first lady? (Actually, that last of these is easily answered. Arthur's wife, Nell, died of pneumonia less than two years before he became president.) President Arthur did ask his sister to assume some social duties and help him care for the youngest of his two children, who was then eleven. He also had installed a stained glass window in Saint John's Episcopal Church, across the street from the White House, in memory of his wife. The memorial window, which exists today, was lit at night so the president could look at it.

Before he entered politics, Chester Arthur was principal of North Pownal Academy, in the southeast corner of Vermont. Later, as a politician, he was often accused of cronyism. In his powerful position as collector of the Port of New York, for example, he hired many more employees than were needed, most of them loyal Republican Party workers. As both vice president and president, however, he established a reputation for independence. Although his party vigorously opposed civil service reform, he asked for and received legislation that established a Civil Service Commission.

Even so, as historian Bernard Weisberger tells us, President Arthur's inclinations were more Victorian than most, and after establishing a ten-to-four workday and a five-day workweek, he was able to indulge his taste for fine foods, wine, and cigars. (He is said to have had a wardrobe of eighty pairs of pants.) And when the Supreme Court gutted 1875 legislation guaranteeing blacks equal protection, the president gave no support to proposed new antisegregation legislation.

# A Vermont Fable

Former Fairfield resident, Robert O'Connor recalls this story:

The Irish potato famine of the 1840s produced a crop of Irish farmers who, for some reason, migrated to Fairfield en masse to hardscrabble dairy farms and the sugar bush and are established there to this date.

The disappointment in their land was soon conquered by a stoic quality probably unique in the race, which brings me to the anecdote about a family—we'll call them the Harrigans—who after six generations were still milking in the 1930s.

One early morning the sixth grandpa was seated at table after breakfast when a grandson appeared breathless at the door. Grandpa looked up from his bowl of maple syrup.

"Grandpa, the barn's on fire!" said the lad.

Grandpa Harrigan put his spoon down, looked out the window, and shook his head. "It never did that before," he said.

Shortly after he became president, Chester A. Arthur discovered that he suffered from a fatal kidney disease. He died in 1886 at the age of fifty-seven, a year and one-half after leaving office.

Directions: To visit the Chester A. Arthur birthplace, on U.S. Route 7, after coming to Fairfield, go north approximately 1 mile and bear right at the fork. Continue 5 miles to the historic site. The road will turn to gravel. The site is open July 4 through mid-October on Saturday and Sunday, 11:00 a.m. to 5:00 p.m. Donations are appreciated. For more information visit www.historicvermont.org/sites/html/arthur.html or call (802) 828-3051.

⋆ ⋆ ⋆ ⋆ ⋆ ⋆ ⋆ ⋆ ⋆ ⋆ ⋆ ⋆ ⋆ ⋆ ⋆ ⋆ ⋆ ⋆ ⋆ ⋆ ⋆ ⋆ ⋆ ⋆ ⋆ ⋆ ⋆ ⋆ ⋆ ⋆

## Vermont's Islands in the Sun—and Sometimes Snow
### Grand Isle County

The advice from insiders is that "most Vermonters know there are places you just don't go in the summer because of the predictable crush of tourists." Several destinations covered in *Vermont Curiosities* make this list, by the way: Camel's Hump, Ben & Jerry's factory in Waterbury, downtown Stowe, and Burlington's Church Street, for four. And the Champlain Islands for a fifth.

The major Champlain Islands are South Hero and Grand Isle (actually one island), North Hero, and Isle la Motte. North and South Hero originally were named the Two Heroes by Ethan Allen. He bought the land after the Revolutionary War and parceled grants to a number of other Green Mountain Boys, modestly naming them, it is said, for himself and fellow hero brother Ira. In 1798 Two Heroes was divided into North Hero, Middle Hero (later renamed Grand Isle), and South Hero.

Touring the Champlain Islands, which usually tops the "visit-during-the-summer-at-your-own-risk" list, can be similarly busy, but not overwhelmingly so. Anyway, the views are striking. Before you go, pick up a "Chamber Map and Business Guide for Vermont's Champlain Islands" from a tourist information outlet. Among the objects of interest up there, here are a few worth noting:

*Hyde Log Cabin* (Grand Isle). Jedediah Hyde Jr. fought in the Revolutionary War after enlisting in the Connecticut Grenadiers at age fourteen. He also learned surveying in Rufus Putnam's Corps of Engineers. After the war Hyde and his father, also a captain (and a Battle of Bunker Hill veteran), were assigned the job of surveying Grand Isle and other parts of Vermont. Captain Hyde Sr. bought acreage on Grand Isle and on the mainland to the east, later moving to Hyde Park, which was named after him. Jedediah Jr. remained on Grand Isle and built a cabin there, which was home to various members of his family for 150 years and remains there today. It is considered one of the oldest log cabins in the United States.

Jedediah Hyde and his father, both Revolutionary War veterans, were assigned to survey Grand Isle. The son stayed and built this cabin, one of the oldest of its kind still standing.

In 1945 the Vermont Historical Society bought the cabin and moved it 2 miles to its present location. An agreement with the Grand Isle County Historical Society led to its current function as a meeting place, museum, and information center.

Directions: Follow U.S. Route 2 east through South Hero. Located just north of the village of Grand Isle, on the right, the site is open July 4 through mid-October, Sunday and Saturday, 11:00 a.m.–5:00 p.m. For more information visit http://historicvermont.org/sites/html/hyde.html or call (802) 828-3051.

*Knight Point State Park.* At the southern tip of North Hero is Knight Point State Park. John Knight, first resident and owner of the ferry that ran between Knight Point and Grand Isle, built a home there

that today is a park staff residence. Knight and his family operated the ferry from 1785 until the first bridge opened in 1892. For 15 years, Herrmann's Lipizzaner Stallions spent the better part of July and August entertaining visitors here with their intricate marching routines, but in 2008 they decided instead to follow the Midwest state fair circuit. They may be back, but if not this will focus attention on other worthy attractions in and just south of Knight Point State Park. First, those in the park:

Shakespeare in the Park—Each August the Vermont Shakespeare Company mounts professionally-acted productions such as *The Comedy of Errors, Twelfth Night,* and *A Midsummer Night's Dream.* In 2005 co-directors Jena Necrason and John Nagle left successful New York acting careers to create their new company, which they hope will become a fixture at Knight Point. All performances are staged outdoors, as Shakespeare intended; www.vermontshakespeare.org.

Jazz on a Summer Night—The Islands Center presents jazz performances on the lawn in Knight Point State Park four Tuesday evenings in July. A different group is featured for each session. Picnickers welcome (bring your own blanket). Tickets available at Lake Champlain Islands Chamber of Commerce. (802) 372-8400; www.champlain islands.com.

Directions: Knight Point State Park is just off Route 2 in North Hero, on the north side of the bridge separating Grand Isle from North Hero.

*Grand Isle Lake House* (Grand Isle). The Lake House, one of the most stunning properties on the Champlain Islands, is the setting for two other events on Grand Isle. A three-story Victorian mansion framed by a 12-foot-wide wraparound porch, it rests on a narrow peninsula with unparalleled views of Lake Champlain islands and the Green Mountains. It was built as a hotel in 1903, and donated to the Preservation Trust of Vermont in 1997 after 35 years as a girls' summer camp; www.grandislelakehouse.com.

Vermont Mozart Festival—The Lake House is one of ten locales to host this thirty-five year-old Vermont institution each year. More than 16,000 visitors hear world-class ensembles, string quartets, and soloists at what consistently is named by the Vermont Chamber of Commerce one of the state's top ten summer events. Consult the Web site for dates, times, and admissions for the various venues; www .vtmozart.org.

Vermont Jazz Ensemble—The seventeen-member jazz ensemble makes an annual appearance at the Grand Isle Lake House each August. The group performs largely in "Big Band" style, also playing blues, Latin, rock, and fusion. The Ensemble made its first appearance at a 1976 YMCA Camp Abenaki jazz weekend, and has grown continually in popularity since then. If you like Glenn Miller, Duke Ellington, Count Basie, Stan Kenton, or Woody Herman, you'll love the Vermont Jazz Ensemble. See their Web site for a complete schedule. Admission; www.vermontjazzensemble.com.

Directions: To reach Grand Isle Lake House, go south on Route 2 across the bridge between North Hero and Grand Isle. Take a left on East Shore Road North and continue 0.7 miles. The Lake House is on the right between two stone pillars.

*Chazy Fossil Reef* (Isle La Motte). Get out your GPS . . . and your time machine. We're going back to the last supercontinent—called Pangaea—that existed from, oh, 300 or so million years ago to about 200 million years ago, when it began breaking up into the configuration of continents that exists today. When you look at this ancient landmass, the first thing you notice is that the area now occupied by Vermont is sandwiched between what is now Europe and the eastern edge of North America. The other revelation is that the Green Mountain State is almost on the equator.

Vermont State naturalist Charles W. Johnson tells us that 500-million-year-old fossils of coral, some of the oldest in the world, occur in limestone the length of Lake Champlain. But coral is an animal community

# Alburg's Binational Customs House

In 1781 the Vermont legislature granted to Ira Allen and sixty-four associates the only town in Grand Isle County that was not a Lake Champlain island. This was Alburg, a peninsula connected by bridges to the other island towns. In those days smuggling was known to occur across the Canadian border, especially during Prohibition. Since then the U.S. and Canadian governments have collaborated to build a common customs house along the U.S.–Canada boundary line in Alburg. It is the only customs house operated and maintained by both countries on the entire international border.

of tropical oceans, and these particular coral existed before Pangaea was fully assembled. So how did such creatures come to live in the interior of New England, 200 miles from the ocean, in a climate nearly 180 degrees from tropical? Continental drift and the effects of plate tectonics, that's how. You can learn more in Johnson's book, *The Nature of Vermont* (see the bibliography). You can also find out for yourself with a trip to the Goodsell Ridge Fossil Preserve. Here more than a half dozen outcroppings in a meadow a quarter mile from the lake reveal parts of an ancient coral reef thrust to the surface from many hundreds of feet below. The remains of sponges, trilobites, and other extinct ancestors of today's soft sea sponge, horseshoe crab, and squid, for example, are all on display. A nearby farmhouse serves as the site's research center and museum.

Directions: Take U.S. Route 2 through North Hero to Route 129. Go left through South Alburg across the bridge to Isle La Motte. Take a left on Main Street and go about 2 miles. Take another left on Quarry Road (the stone building on the right houses the Isle La Motte

★ ★ ★ ★ ★ ★ ★ ★ ★ ★ ★ ★ ★ ★ ★ ★ ★ ★ ★ ★ ★ ★ ★ ★ ★ ★ ★ ★ ★ ★ ★

Historical Society). The Goodsell Ridge Preserve is about a half mile farther, on the left side of Quarry Road. The preserve is open dawn to dusk for self-guided tours. Call (802) 862-4150.

### No Place for the Devil in the Old Round Church
Richmond

Right. No corners equals no place for the Devil to hide. That's one theory, anyway, accounting for churches built in this manner. Richmond's Old Round Church doesn't really qualify, because it consists of sixteen sides, which still, of course, leaves corners, albeit pretty skimpy ones.

The Old Round Church was built in 1813 as a nondenominational meetinghouse, with the town's Baptists, Universalists, Congregationalists, and Methodists all sharing the facilities, and all serving as proprietors. The

Some say the Round Church has sixteen sides because builder William Rhodes had seventeen workers—one for each side, and the last for the belfry. Think they backed into that legend?

land was donated by a tavern keeper and a storekeeper, and the church construction costs came to $2,305.42—all raised by the sale of pews.

This church held up for 160 years, when it was closed by state officials as unsafe for public use. In 1976 the church was turned over to the Richmond Historical Society for restoration. Five years and $180,000 later, the church was opened again and has remained so. A second restoration now under way will add a new cedar shingle roof, sprinkler system, handrails to the balcony stairwells, and a paint job inside and out.

Directions: From I-89, take exit 11 and drive east to the center of Richmond Village on U.S. Route 2. At the four corners, turn right and take Bridge Street south. The Old Round Church is on the left, just across the Winooski River, less than 1 mile from the village. The church is open to the public during the summer and fall foliage seasons, 10:00 a.m. to 4:00 p.m. daily. For more information, including a virtual tour, visit www.oldroundchurch.com.

### The Museum That Sugar Built

Shelburne

Everything about the Shelburne Museum is grand. On its forty-five acres are thirty-nine buildings. Twenty-five of them have been moved there from locations up to 200 miles away. For visitors unable or unwilling to walk the grounds, a jitney stands by to transport them to whatever exhibits they fancy.

Shelburne Museum is the creation of Electra Havemeyer Webb, whose father inherited the American Sugar Refinery Company from *his* father and renamed it the Domino Sugar Company. Henry O. Havemeyer was able to leave Electra enough money for any collectible she coveted. Electra's father and mother also passed on to her their own strong collecting habits. Electra knew exactly what she wanted, and from the museum's founding in 1947 until she died in 1960, she had collected some 80,000 items, including valuable impressionist art by Monet, Manet, and Degas she had chosen from her parents' collection. Today the museum is estimated to include 150,000 items.

✮ ✮ ✮ ✮ ✮ ✮ ✮ ✮ ✮ ✮ ✮ ✮ ✮ ✮ ✮ ✮ ✮ ✮ ✮ ✮ ✮ ✮ ✮ ✮ ✮ ✮ ✮ ✮ ✮ ✮

Let's sample the curiosities. Probably most dramatic is the *Ticonderoga*, a hundred-year-old side-paddle-wheel passenger steamboat—the last to operate commercially on Lake Champlain. This National Historic Landmark was still in service and about to be scrapped when historian Ralph N. Hill's crusade to "Save the *Ti*" led him to Electra Havemeyer Webb. She bought it as an excursion boat in 1951, but when that enterprise failed, she decided to move the ship overland 2 miles to the museum, a monumental task on its own. First a basin

Here's the scene as Arnold Graton looked on helplessly from the second helicopter as the silo is being lowered.

was dug adjacent to the lake and a cradle was built in it on a slightly higher level. The 220-foot-long, 292-ton *Ticonderoga* was floated into the lower level of the basin, which was then dammed up and the water level raised. The *Ti* then floated over the cradle and the water was drained from the basin to create the first leg of a roadway. This was slow going. Workers had to continually retrieve from the stern the 300 feet of track laid to ease the *Ti* along, only to lay it again forward, in the ship's path. As a result, sixty-five days were spent moving it to

★ ★ ★ ★ ★ ★ ★ ★ ★ ★ ★ ★ ★ ★ ★ ★ ★ ★ ★ ★ ★ ★ ★ ★ ★ ★ ★ ★ ★ ★

a final resting place. If you spend a half hour or more aboard, though, you'll agree it was well worth the effort (especially if you remind yourself you weren't a member of the moving crew).

One building added to the collection after Electra's death is difficult to miss. The Round Barn probably will be the first building you see after entering the museum grounds. Built 50 miles away in East Passumpsic, Vermont, in 1901, late in 1985 it was dismantled, plank by numbered-and-lettered plank and transported to Shelburne by a convoy of flatbed trucks.

That was the simple part. A 9,000-pound wooden silo, the core of the barn, was judged to be too fragile to make the trip by truck. An airlift was funded by grants from Pratt & Whitney and the Sikorsky companies, and on March 11, 1986, a Skycrane helicopter made the journey from East Passumpsic to Shelburne—but not without a few uneasy moments on what turned out to be a windy ninety-minute trip. Arnold Graton, the New Hampshire contractor who supervised the barn move and restored the structure to museum specifications, rode shotgun in a second helicopter. As they went over Camel's Hump, Arnold noticed that because of the wind, the silo was swinging, and stretched taut straight behind the copter rather than hanging directly below. Just as they passed the peak, he was aghast to see one of the sixteen primary cables attached to the silo snap loose; then a few minutes later a second cable broke away, and then a third. Arnold's copter landed less than a minute before the silo copter, and he raced to the landing site just in time to help workers on the ground guide the 29-foot-high, 20-foot-diameter silo into place. "It got a bit dicey there toward the end," recalled Arnold by phone. "That wind was whipping over Camel's Hump."

By coincidence the Pratt & Whitney employee who suggested using a Skycrane was the barn builder's granddaughter. Bernice Quimby, a thirty-seven-year employee of United Technologies Pratt & Whitney Division, grew up less than a mile from the barn. Her carpenter grandfather, Fred "Silo" Quimby, had built three round barns.

The one in East Passumpsic, donated to the museum by its owners, was the last one standing.

In aggregate, the variety of exhibits in the museum's buildings will gratify the broadest of tastes. Electra's personal preferences ran to folk art, which, as she defined it, is the work of untaught men and women who made useful things—beautiful because they have both a certain directness and simplicity and relate to their surroundings. This describes most of the Shelburne's exhibits, including the quilts, art, weathervanes, textiles, furniture, tools, toys, vehicles, and glass walking sticks. To make the best use of your time, take advantage of the museum's two-day admittance with a full-price admission.

The Museum Café offers a variety of fresh and delicious menu items, using local Vermont ingredients, when available. Wraps, panini, pasta, salads, and a variety of sandwiches are served both inside and from an outdoor grill.

Directions: From I-89 north, take the South Burlington exit. Go south on U.S. Route 7 for 7 miles, to the village of Shelburne, and look for the sign on the right. The museum is open daily, 10:00 am to 5:00 pm, mid-May through October. For more information go to www.shelburnemuseum.org or call (802) 985-3346.

Shelburne Farms: Two miles from the museum, at Harbor and Bay Roads, is Shelburne Farms, built by Dr. William Steward Webb and his wife, Lila, Electra's in-laws. Today the 1889 mansion serves as a twenty-five-bedroom inn and is surrounded by a 1,000-acre farm now run by two Webb grandsons as a nonprofit organization dedicated to agricultural conservation and education. For more information visit www.shelburnefarms.org or call (802) 985-8686.

### "Reverence"—A Dream Come True, Big Time
South Burlington

Driving north along I-89 between exits 12 and 13, look for an unexpected sight on your right: the tails of two whales, 13 feet long, diving into a sea of grass. The inspiration for Jim Sardonis's striking 1989

Sardonis's *Reverence* was inspired by the 1998 Alaska oil spill.

sculpture was a dream. "I was standing on a beach," says Jim, "and these two whale tails came up, with the water pouring off. And I woke up thinking this would make a great sculpture. At first I thought of a fountain setting, but it soon evolved into using the ground as an imaginary ocean surface, and allowing people to get right up to it and feel the scale a little bit more. After being commissioned to create the sculpture, I went out on a couple of whale watches to observe humpbacks. It was very inspiring."

The two whales, which took Jim nine months to complete, were made from thirty-six tons of Impala black granite imported from South Africa. The two finished pieces total roughly ten tons and are anchored by stainless steel pins in a 5-foot-deep concrete foundation. Each tail consists of two pieces joined just below the flukes.

Because of the aggregate size and weight, Jim's studio was too small to accommodate the work. He arranged for space at Granite Imports, as well as use of their thirty-ton forklifts, overhead cranes, and a variety of diamond saws, and supervised a team of experienced granite artisans in the early stages of the process. The first step was to cut through the two 4-foot-thick blocks, using an 11-foot-diameter circular saw. Each of these cuts took several hours. In later stages Jim used his own handheld 9-inch saw along with pneumatic hammers, chisels, and grinders.

The sculpture was originally commissioned by a British metals trader who at the time lived in Randolph, Vermont. But financing fell through, and after ten years, the sculpture was sold and moved 60 miles north to be the centerpiece of the proposed Technology Sculpture Park. Passersby that day were treated to a once-in-a-lifetime sight: two granite whales migrating north on a flatbed truck.

While Jim was working on the whale tails, which he had named *Pas de deux,* the Exxon Valdez oil spill in Alaska made headlines worldwide. Jim decided to use his work to raise people's consciousness about environmental issues. As a result he renamed his work *Reverence* and has completed a number of sculptures in this vein, among them those of several extinct species—passenger pigeons and great auks, for example. Currently, Jim is working on a sculpture of a group of polar bears for a library in Andover, Massachusetts, intended to highlight some of the effects of global warming. Somebody out there is paying attention, and doing something about it.

Directions: From I-89 exit 12, take a right at the end of the ramp, then right again at the first light. Drive 2 to 3 miles past a couple of shopping centers to the Technology Sculpture Park sign on the left. Turn left, drive halfway around the circular drive, and park. Walk across the field toward I-89. The sculpture is on the highest point of surrounding land.

For more of Jim's work visit www.sardonis.com.

# bibliography

Beckley, Hosea. *The History of Vermont.* Brattleboro, VT: George H. Salisbury, 1846.

Cheney, Cora, and Robert Maclean. *Vermont: The State with the Storybook Past.* Shelburne, VT: The New England Press, 1996.

Cohn, Arthur. *Lake Champlain's Sailing Canal Boats.* Basin Harbor, VT: Lake Champlain Maritime Museum, 2003.

Dodge, Bertha S. *Tales of Vermont: Ways and People.* Shelburne, VT: The New England Press, 1996.

Duffy, John J., Samuel B. Hand, and Ralph H. Orth, eds. *The Vermont Encyclopedia.* Burlington: University of Vermont Press, 2003.

Goodman, Lee Dana. *Vermont Saints and Sinners.* Shelburne, VT: The New England Press, 1985.

Graff, Chris. *Dateline Vermont.* North Pomfret, VT: Thistle Hill Publications, 2006.

Holman, Jordan D. Jr., and Castleton State College History Students. *Beautiful Lake Bomoseen.* Castleton, VT: Castleton State College, 1999.

Johnson, Charles W. *The Nature of Vermont: Introduction and Guide to a New England Environment.* Hanover, NH: University Press of New England, 1998.

Klyza, Christopher, and Stephen Trombulak. *The Story of Vermont.* Hanover, NH: University Press of New England, 1999.

Pettengill, Helen. *History of Grafton, Vermont.* Grafton, VT: Grafton Historical Society, 1975.

Rogak, Lisa. *Stones and Bones of New England.* Guilford, CT: Globe Pequot Press, 2004.

Rogers, Barbara, and Stillman Rogers. *Vermont: Off the Beaten Path,* 6th ed. Guilford, CT: Globe Pequot Press, 2004.

Sherman, Joe. *Fast Lane on a Dirt Road.* White River Junction, VT: Chelsea Green Publishing Company, 2000.

Strickland, Ron, and Chris Bohjalian. *Vermonters: Oral Histories.* Hanover, NH: University Press of New England, 1998.

*Vermont Atlas & Gazetteer,* 11th ed. Yarmouth, ME: DeLorme, 2003.

Waterman, Laura, and Guy Waterman. *Forest and Crag.* Boston: Appalachian Mountain Club Books, 2003.

Wheeler, Scott. *Rumrunners and Revenuers.* Shelburne, VT: The New England Press, 2002.

# appendix

★ ★ ★ ★ ★ ★ ★ ★ ★ ★ ★ ★ ★ ★ ★ ★ ★ ★ ★ ★ ★ ★ ★ ★ ★ ★ ★

## Organizing Your Curiosities Tours

Because *Vermont Curiosities* entries are listed alphabetically in the text, we've compiled lists of them below based on direct-line travel, by highway. This way, whether you're arriving from out-of-state or are already here, you can use these lists as a two-dimensional global positioning system to plot your day's travels.

As an arbitrary organizer, all routes run either from south to north or from west to east. Entries listed are within 10 miles of the respective route. Specific directions can be found at the end of each text entry. Some event-driven entries are tied to specific dates. These entries are asterisked.

### Interstate 91 (or the more leisurely U.S. Route 5)

Fort Dummer, First Nontribal Settlement
 Brattleboro   Ch. 2

*Strolling of the Heifers
 Brattleboro   Ch. 2

*Latchis Hotel and Theatre
 Brattleboro   Ch. 2

British Indian Yankee . . . (Rudyard Kipling home)
 Dummerston   Ch. 2

"Taste Delights" (Curtis's Barbecue)
 Putney   Ch. 2

Indian Cliff Paintings
 Bellows Falls   Ch. 2

Hetty Green
 Bellows Falls   Ch. 2

First U.S. Canal
 Bellows Falls   Ch. 2

Percussion Instruments to the Stars
 Gageville   Ch. 2

Major Angas (Inn at Saxtons River)
 Saxtons River   Ch. 2

Last Dairy Farm in Rockingham
 Rockingham   Ch. 2

# appendix

America's Smallest State Capital
    Montpelier          Ch. 6

Who Sculpted Little Margaret?
    Montpelier          Ch. 6

*Ben & Jerry's Flavor Graveyard and Factory
    Waterbury          Ch. 6

Old Round Church
    Richmond           Ch. 9

Reverence (Whale's Tails)
    South Burlington    Ch. 9

ECHO Center and Museum
    Burlington          Ch. 9

*Flynn Performance Center
    Burlington          Ch. 9

Perkins Museum (woolly mammoth tusk)
    Burlington          Ch. 5

Hyde Log Cabin
    Grand Isle          Ch. 9

Chazy Fossils
    Isle La Motte       Ch. 9

President Arthur's Birthplace
    Fairfield           Ch. 9

Swanton (Vermont's largest Abenaki settlement)
    Swanton             Ch. 8

## U.S. Route 7

Black World War II Museum
    Pownal              Ch. 3

Covered Bridge Museum
    Bennington          Ch. 3

Grandma Moses Heist (Bennington Museum)
    Bennington          Ch. 3

Robert Frost Stone House Museum
    Shaftsbury          Ch. 3

Lincoln Family Home at Hildene
    Manchester          Ch. 3

New England Maple Museum
    Pittsford           Ch. 5

# appendix

Wilson Castle
    Proctor               Ch. 5

Marble Museum
    Proctor               Ch. 5

Queen Connie (Gorilla lifting Volkswagen)
    Brandon              Ch. 5

Bread Loaf; Robert Frost Wayside Area and Trail
    Ripton               Ch. 7

Horse-Drawn Garbage and Recycling Truck
    Bristol               Ch. 7

Smallest, Oldest Vermont City
    Vergennes         Ch. 7

Lake Champlain Maritime Museum
    Ferrisburgh       Ch. 7

Rokeby Underground Railroad Museum
    Ferrisburgh       Ch. 7

Shelburne Museum
    Shelburne         Ch. 9

**State Route 100**

Phineas Gage Incident
    Cavendish         Ch. 4

President Coolidge birthplace
    Plymouth Notch   Ch. 4

Ben & Jerry's Flavor Graveyard and Factory
    Waterbury         Ch. 6

Trapp Family Lodge (Maria von Trapp story)
    Stowe             Ch. 6

Climbing Mount Mansfield (from Long Trail story)
    Stowe             Ch. 1

*Rusty Nail Bar and Grill (Ice Bar)
    Stowe             Ch. 6

# index

# index

# index

# index

# about the author

⭐ ⭐ ⭐ ⭐ ⭐ ⭐ ⭐ ⭐ ⭐ ⭐ ⭐ ⭐ ⭐ ⭐ ⭐ ⭐ ⭐ ⭐ ⭐ ⭐ ⭐ ⭐ ⭐ ⭐ ⭐ ⭐ ⭐ ⭐ ⭐ ⭐ ⭐

Robert F. Wilson has worked as a promotion writer for *Reader's Digest*; and as an editor for McGraw-Hill, Houghton Mifflin, Macmillan, Scholastic, and the sadly swallowed Silver Burdett. In his younger days, under the unfortunate pseudonym Pamela S. Bell, Wilson was National Secretary for Scholastic's Teen Age Book Club, during which time he took numerous member phone calls in falsetto. He has written twelve books, several of which are still in print.

Wilson makes the following offer: Bring a copy of this book to his home in Saxtons River, and he will not only sign it but will provide milk and cookies. Finally, as a public service, Wilson has sworn never again to refer to himself in the third person, beginning . . . *now*.

# about the photographer

⭐ ⭐ ⭐ ⭐ ⭐ ⭐ ⭐ ⭐ ⭐ ⭐ ⭐ ⭐ ⭐ ⭐ ⭐ ⭐ ⭐ ⭐ ⭐ ⭐ ⭐ ⭐ ⭐ ⭐ ⭐ ⭐ ⭐ ⭐ ⭐ ⭐ ⭐

Victoria Blewer left the chaos and the clutter of New York City in 1986 to devote herself full time to fine art photography in the hills of Vermont. She works entirely in black-and-white, and then hand-colors the images. Her work has been featured in full-length photo essays in the *Boston Globe* Sunday Magazine, *Vermont Life,* and *Vermont Magazine.*